# The Wealth of Nations

## A Summary of
### Adam Smith's original work

## by David Smith

*The Wealth of Nations 100 page summaries*
copyright © by 100 page summaries.

All rights reserved.
Printed in the United States of America.

ISBN: 978-1-939370-10-5

Library of Congress Cataloging-in-Publication Data

David Smith
The Wealth of Nations A Summary of Adam Smith's original work

This publication is designed to provide accurate and authoritative information in regard to the subject matter covered. It is sold with the understanding that neither the author nor the publisher is a registered expert in the subject matter discussed. If legal advice or other expert assistance is required, the services of a competent professional person should be sought.

# Table of Contents

# Introduction and Plan of the Work

A nation's labor provides it with its needs and wants. These will be in the form of either the actual product produced from that labor, or an item purchased as a result of trading that product with other nations.

The first book covers the subject of improving the productive powers of labor.

The second book treats the nature of capital.

The third book addresses the issue of Europe's policies being more favorable towards industry within towns than towards agriculture.

The fourth book explains the differences in political economy theories on the importance of industry in towns and in the countryside.

The fifth book describes the revenue of the sovereign, or commonwealth.

# Book I

Of the Causes of Improvement in the Productive Powers of Labor, and of the Order According to Which its Produce is Naturally Distributed Among the Different Ranks of the People

## CHAPTER I
### Of the Division of Labor

### Summary:

The greatest improvements in the productive power of labor, as well as the development of specialized skills, dexterity, and judgment, occur when there is division of labor (specialization).

Let us look at the example of a pin-maker. An unskilled tradesman could perhaps produce one pin a day. But if we divide the work involved into a number of different trades—one man draws out the wire, another straightens it, a third cuts it, a fourth points it, etc.—separating the production of the pin into about eighteen distinct operations, then ten men could produce 48,000 pins in a day.

There are three reasons for this exponential increase in productivity:

Firstly, this division of labor increases each workman's dexterity; since each man is working on a sole task, his specialized knowledge of that task will grow, thus increasing his dexterity.

Secondly, division of labor in this way will save time for each worker. Since the worker is focusing on an individual task, he does not have to pass from one task to another in order to change tools, for example. This will save time and thus increase each worker's productivity.

Thirdly, workers who spend large amounts of time on a single, repetitive operation often come up with ideas for machines to streamline the equipment and tools used, thus increasing productivity. Further improvements have been made thanks to the ingenuity of the manufacturers of these machines.

# CHAPTER II
## Of the Principle Which Gives
## Occasion to the Division of Labor

### Summary:

The division of labor came about as a result of our preference, as human beings, for bartering and exchanging items. Trading items is part of human nature, and common to every society.

Man will always need help from others. He will be more likely to receive that help, however, if he can turn others' self-interest to his advantage, by showing them that there is something in it for them. The butcher, brewer and baker who sell us our dinner are not motivated to do so by kindness, but by their own self-interest.

Nobody but a beggar chooses to depend solely upon the benevolence of his fellow citizens. Most of our needs are met through bartering and purchasing. This is what originally gave rise to the introduction of division of labor.

# CHAPTER III
## That the Division of Labor Is Limited by the Extent of the Market

### Summary:

In areas in which the market is very small, the division of labor tends to be limited, with workers often needing to do several jobs rather than focusing on a single trade or task. In a small village, for example, a farmer will often act as the butcher, baker and brewer for his own family.

Let us compare the transportation of goods between London and Edinburgh by land versus by ship. By ship, it would take only six to eight men to transport the same quantity of goods as it would take 100 men, fifty wagons and 400 horses to transport by land. As for expenses, transporting 200 tons of goods by land from London to Edinburgh would incur costs for the upkeep of 100 men and 400 horses for three weeks, as well as the wear and tear to the fifty wagons. Expenses for transportation by water would be for the upkeep of only six to eight men and the wear and tear caused to the ship by the cargo. To this we must add the difference in insurance costs for transport via land versus water.

Plantations in North American colonies have consistently been planted along shorelines or riverbanks.

# CHAPTER IV
## Of the Origin and Use of Money

### Summary:

Once division of labor has been implemented within a society, the members of that society will start to trade.

When division of labor was first employed, initial experiences in trade and exchange must have been difficult and often impractical. One man has more of a commodity than he needs; another has less. The former would be glad to dispose of, and the latter to purchase—but if the latter has nothing the former needs, no exchange can be made.

In primitive society, for example, cattle were the common commodity used for commerce; in Abyssinia, it was salt. So the man who wished to buy salt but had nothing other than cattle to give in exchange would have been obliged to buy salt to the value of a whole ox.

This led to the idea of a common currency in the form of metal. This had its inconveniences, however, in terms of weighing and evaluating values. To prevent abuse, countries started to stamp specific quantities onto the metals—which later led to coinage and minting. Coins displayed a stamp on either side confirming the coin's purity and weight.

The word "value" has two different meanings: it can refer to an object's utility or its purchasing power. The former could be called "value in use;" the latter "value in exchange." Water is valuable in the sense that it is essential to the preservation of life, but its purchasing power is very low.

# CHAPTER V
## Of the Real and Nominal Price of Commodities, or of their Price in Labor, and their Price in Money

### Summary:

An individual's wealth is determined by his capacity to provide for the wants and needs of human life. With division of labor, an individual man's labor provides for only a portion of these wants and needs. As such, an individual's wealth is in fact determined by the amount of labor he can afford to purchase.

The value of a commodity to a man who owns it but does not intend to use it himself is equal to the quantity of labor he can purchase with it. Labor is the real measure of the trading value of all commodities. The value of a commodity to a man who wants either to dispose of it or trade it for something else is the labor it can save him.

Although it is said that wealth is power, it does not follow that a wealthy individual is a powerful individual. He can acquire power by purchasing either labor or the commodities produced through labor. A man's wealth is thus determined by the amount of other men's labor he is able to purchase.

Although labor is the true determinant of a commodity's value, it is in fact money which ultimately determines an item's worth. This is because a commodity's value is calculated according to its exchangeable value; i.e, the quantity of *money*—as opposed to the quantity of *labor*—for which it can be exchanged.

The amount of labor required to purchase a commodity remains constant, although this same amount of labor may purchase a greater or lesser quantity of commodities. It is the price of the commodity that changes, not the value of the labor. Though equal quantities of labor are always of equal value to the worker, to the person who employs him, the price of labor seems to vary, like that of all other things.

Labor, like all commodities, has a real and a nominal price. Its real price relates to the quantity of needs and wants it can purchase; its nominal price relates to the amount of money. The worker is rich or poor in proportion to the real—not the nominal—price of his labor.

The real price of a commodity will remain at the same value; the nominal price may vary considerably depending on fluctuations in the value of gold and silver.

Labor is the only universal measure of value, or the only standard by which we can compare the values of different commodities, at all times, and in all places.

Since it is the nominal or money price of goods that regulates almost anything to do with price, it is not surprising that this aspect is focused on more than real price.

It is difficult to accurately equate the price of labor. On the other hand, the price of a commodity such as corn, although not regularly recorded throughout history, is generally better known and frequently referred to by historians and other writers.

Commercial nations subsequently developed coins from the metals they used as currency: gold for larger payments, silver for purchases of moderate value, and copper, or some other coarse metal, for the smallest.

The Romans are said to have initially had nothing but copper money, which appears to have continued as the measure of value in that republic. The northern nations seem to have used silver from the outset, with silver coins still used in Britain in the time of the Saxons. There was little gold coined, however, until the time of Edward III, nor any copper till that of James I.

# CHAPTER VI
## Of the Component Part of the Price of Commodities

### Summary:

In early society, it appears that the amount of labor required to purchase an object was the only basis for exchanging objects. As such, a product that took two days of labor to produce was worth double a product requiring one day of labor. The former would also be more valued due to the higher level of complexity and dexterity involved. In later society, labor requiring greater skill was acknowledged in the form of wages of labor.

Once stock is built up, some individuals invest it in employing workers, with a view to adding further value to their merchandise. The value these workmen add to the commodity is then used to pay their wages, with the remainder being profit on stock for the employer.

The real value of the different component parts of price is measured by the amount of labor an individual can purchase. In addition, rent and profit are also components of the price of a commodity.

In every modern society, the price of a commodity reflects these three component parts. In the price of corn, for example, one part pays the rent of the landlord, another pays the wages and maintenance of the workers and animals, and the third is the profit made by the farmer. These three parts make up the whole price of corn. A fourth part is used to replenish the farmer's stock or to compensate the wear and tear of his laboring animals and other farm equipment.

As a commodity undergoes more manufacturing processes, the part of the price which represents wages and profit increases in proportion to rent. In the process of manufacture, every subsequent profit is greater than the previous.

Wages, profit and rent are the three original sources of all revenue, as well as of all exchangeable value. All other revenue is ultimately derived from one of these sources.

# Chapter VII
## Of the Natural and Market Price of Commodities

## Summary:

In every society, there is an average rate for wages, profit, and rent, determined by the society's circumstances and the nature of each employment. These average rates are known as natural rates. If the price of a commodity equals the total costs of its production, it is then sold for what is known as its "natural price"—or the cost incurred to bring it to market.

The actual price at which a commodity is sold is known as its market price. This is determined by the quantity of the commodity brought to market and the demand for that commodity. Those purchasing the commodity could be referred to as the "effectual demanders," and their demand the "effectual demand," since this demand may be sufficient to *effectuate* the bringing of the commodity to market.

If the quantity of a commodity brought to market falls short of the effectual demand, those wishing to purchase that commodity will be willing to pay more, and consequently the market price will rise.

If the quantity of a commodity brought to market exceeds the effectual demand, it cannot all be sold to those willing to pay the whole value; a portion will need to be sold to those wishing to pay less. This lower price will reduce the price of the whole, and as such the market price will fall.

The natural price of a commodity is the base price to which prices continually gravitate; despite the factors affecting them, prices will constantly return and align with the natural price.

The same number of agricultural workers may produce different quantities of a commodity each year. Only an average produce by an industry can be suited to effectual demand.

Manufacturing secrets are often better kept than trade secrets. When an individual or trading company has a monopoly over the supply of a commodity, this is as effective as having a manufacturing or trade secret. This will generally raise the market price of a particular commodity above its natural price.

# Chapter VIII
## Of the Wages of Labor

### Summary:

The wages of labor consist of what the labor produces.

As soon as land becomes private property, the landlord requests a share of the produce.

In the manufacturing trade, workmen need an employer to supply the materials, their wages and maintenance. The employer benefits from the value added to the materials by the workmen, and this is his profit.

Wages of labor are governed by the contract signed between the two parties, with workmen aiming to gain as much as possible, and employers aiming to give as little as possible. Under the law, employers are allowed to join forces, whereas workmen are not. There are no acts of parliament against joining forces to lower the price of work, but many against joining forces to raise it.

Wages cannot be reduced below a certain rate, even for the most menial types of labor. As a general guide, the lowest-paid workers must earn at least double the cost of their own maintenance in order to bring up two children. Since half of all children die before reaching adulthood, a man should aim to have at least four children, in the hope that two may live to that age. The upkeep for four children may be nearly equal to that for one man.

A wealthy man with an income high enough to cover the upkeep of his family will employ servants. An independent worker with sufficient stock to purchase the materials for his own work and pay for his upkeep will himself employ workers, in order to make a profit from their work.

A steady increase in a society's revenue will result in a consistent rise in wages. Wages are significantly higher in North America than in Britain: in 1773, workers in the province of New York earned more than workers in London, despite the fact that provisions are much lower in North America than in Britain. North America, although not as rich as Britain, is heading faster towards the acquisition of wealth.

The most indicative sign of a country's prosperity is the increase in number of inhabitants. The number of inhabitants in the British colonies in North America doubled within twenty years; labor in this region is so well rewarded that having numerous children was viewed as a source of prosperity rather than a burden to the parents.

The price of bread and meat is the same throughout the United Kingdom, but wages in large towns are frequently twenty percent higher than those in surrounding, smaller towns. A poor workman who is able to afford the upkeep of his family in an area in which wages are low would be affluent if he lived in an area in which wages are high.

It is difficult to accurately ascertain wages of labor, since wages can differ even within the same workplace and for the same sort of labor, depending not only on the workers' skills but also the employer's fair-mindedness.

Over time, the real quantity of wants and needs that can be purchased with labor has increased in greater proportion than its money price. Grain is cheaper, potatoes cost half the price; turnips, carrots and cabbages are all widely produced. Improved manufacturing has led to widespread availability of good-quality, reasonably priced linen and woolen clothing, as well as cheaper and better-quality tools and equipment.

No society can flourish if the majority of its citizens are miserable. Those who employ and as such feed, clothe, and lodge the majority of a society's people should have a share of the produce of their own labor, to ensure that they themselves are well-fed, clothed, and lodged.

Poverty does not prevent people from getting married—and, indeed, seems to go hand in hand with a higher number of children in families. A half-starved Highland woman will often have over twenty children, while wealthier women are often unable to conceive or are exhausted by two or three children. But poverty is not conducive to raising children; it is not uncommon for a mother who has given birth to twenty children to have only two of them alive. In some cases, half of children die before reaching the age of four—and in almost all cases before the age of ten. These high mortality rates are particularly prevalent amongst children of families from poorer backgrounds who cannot afford to care for them as well as their wealthier counterparts. Population figures are regulated by these deaths; on the other hand, the demand for men, as for any other commodity, regulates the production of men.

Men will always be more active in employment for which wages are high as opposed to low. The wages of labor are regulated by the demand for labor and sustenance costs. The demand for labor determines the quantity of needs and wants that a worker will be able to purchase, with wages of labor being determined by what is needed to purchase this quantity. In times of abundance, demand for labor increases and wages therefore increase; whereas in times of scarcity, wages will decrease.

# Chapter IX
## Of the Profits of Stock

### Summary:

Fluctuations in profits of stock (assets) are influenced by the same factors that cause fluctuations in wages of labor and a society's wealth; however, these factors affect one and the other very differently.

Increased stock (assets) will raise wages and lower profit. Competition between merchants tends to lower profit.

Although we can measure average wages, it is difficult to measure profits as they are affected by fluctuations in commodity prices as well as by competition. It may be possible, however, to estimate average profits of stock based on interest rates; as interest rates fluctuate, so do profits of stock.

Generally, more stock is required to trade within a large town than within a village. Profits in the large town will be lower than those in the village due to the higher number of competitors in the town. Wages will generally be higher in a large town than in a country village. In a thriving town, merchants with large amounts of stock often cannot find sufficient workmen and therefore bid against one another, which raises wages and lowers profits.

Wages of labor, interest rates, and consequently the profits of stock are higher in North American and West Indian colonies than they are in Britain. With more land than stock to cultivate, any stock employed in the purchase and improvement of such land must yield a very large profit; consequently, profitable employment enables the landowner to increase the number of staff he is able to pay a good wage.

The lowest rate of profit must always be more than sufficient to compensate for the occasional losses incurred when employing stock. This surplus amount is the only clear profit. In the case of borrowing money, the interest a borrower can afford to pay is measured according to the clear profit. The lowest interest rate must be more than sufficient to compensate for the occasional losses incurred by the lender.

Interest rates generally fluctuate in relation to this rate of clear profit, as profit rises or falls. In the case of a clear profit of 8% to 10%, it would be reasonable, in the case of a business loan, for half of it to go to interest.

The price of work tends to increase more in line with high profits than it does high wages. The rise of profit operates like compound interest; merchants often complain about the bad effects of high wages in terms of increased prices, yet say nothing about the bad effects of high profits.

# Chapter X
## Of Wages and Profit in the Different Employments of Labor and Stock

### Summary:

The advantages and disadvantages of various employments of labor and stock, within a specific geographical area, are either equal or continually tend toward equality.

### Part I

Inequalities arising from the nature of employments themselves

Wages vary according to the level of difficulty or unpleasantness of a job. A tailor, for example, earns less than a weaver since his work is much easier. A blacksmith seldom earns as much in twelve hours as a coal miner does in eight; his work is just as dirty but is less dangerous, is carried out in daylight, and above ground. Disagreeableness and disgrace affect the profits of stock in the same manner as the wages of labor. A pub landlord is exposed to the brutality of every drunkard—yet there is no other trade in which a small stock yields such a large profit.

Wages also vary according to the level of expense and difficulty involved in learning the business. When a business owner invests in expensive machinery, he expects to recover his investment as well as make a profit from the extraordinary work performed by the machine during its life cycle. A man trained for a job that requires extraordinary dexterity and skill, at the expense of time and effort on the part of the employer, may be compared to one of these expensive machines.

During an apprenticeship, the apprentice's labor belongs to his master, but his upkeep is still the responsibility of his parents. The master is generally paid for teaching him his trade. It is reasonable, therefore, that the wages of skilled mechanics should be higher than those of general workers.

Employment is more constant in some trades than others. In manufacturing, for example, a journeyman can be pretty sure of finding employment throughout the year. A mason or bricklayer, on the other hand, cannot work during bad weather. Consequently, the bricklayer's wage must be sufficient to ensure his subsistence during the idle periods.

Wages vary according to the amount of trust which must be placed in an employee; for example, goldsmiths' and jewelers' wages are superior to those of many other employees, on account of the precious materials with which they are entrusted.

Wages also vary according to the probability or improbability of success in a job; for example, the probability of employment in mechanics' trades is almost certain, whereas it is very uncertain in the liberal professions—for a lawyer the odds are 20:1 against success.

In order to succeed in the insurance business, premiums must be sufficient to compensate for losses, cover administrative and management costs, and guarantee a better profit than would have been made from an equal investment in another trade.

The ordinary rate of profit always rises more or less with the risk. It does not, however, seem to rise in proportion to it.

A pharmacist's job is much more agreeable than that of a craftsman, and the trust placed in the former is of much greater importance. His profit, however, will generally be no more than the reasonable wages of labor.

Retail goods are generally much cheaper in major towns than in country villages. It costs no more to transport grocery goods to a major town than it does to a country village—but it costs a great deal more to transport corn and cattle.

Fortunes are sometimes made through speculation. The speculative merchant may be a corn merchant this year, a wine merchant the next, and so on. Although a speculator may make a considerable fortune with two or three successful speculations, he is just as likely to lose.

When an entrepreneur attempts to establish a new business, he first needs to attract workmen by offering higher wages than they might earn elsewhere in their trades. Setting up a new business always involves a certain amount of speculation, with the entrepreneur hoping to make extraordinary profits.

The demand for farm labor is greater during the hay-mowing and harvest periods than throughout the rest of the year, and consequently wages rise with the demand. During wartime, when fifty thousand or so sailors were forced from the merchant service into that of the king, the demand for sailors on merchant ships rose with their scarcity—as did their wages.

All commodities are subject to price fluctuations. In some employments, the same quantity of industry will always produce the same quantity of commodities; but there are other employments in which the same quantity of industry will not always produce the same quantity of commodities; for example, agriculture. The price of a commodity, therefore, can vary not only in line with demand, but in line with quantity. Speculators will buy commodities when they expect their prices to rise, and sell them when the price is likely to fall.

## Part II

Inequalities occasioned by policies in Europe

The (prevailing) policy in Europe causes inequalities in three ways:

by restraining competition in certain employments to a smaller number than would otherwise be likely to enter into them;

by increasing competition in others beyond what it naturally would be;

by obstructing the free circulation of labor and stock, both from employment to employment and from place to place.

First: The exclusive privileges of corporations restrain competition.

In order to practice a trade in a town, a person is required to have carried out an apprenticeship in that town, under a qualified master. Corporations' bylaws regulate the number of apprentices any master is allowed to train, and the number of years each apprentice is required to serve. The intention is to restrain competition to a smaller number. In Europe, the general duration of an apprenticeship is seven years.

The patrimony of a poor man lies in the strength and dexterity of his hands, and to hinder him from employing this strength and dexterity is a violation of human rights, both of the workman and of potential employers. Even the longest apprenticeship, however, does not provide security against fraud; customers are more reassured by a sterling mark on a plate or a stamp on linen and woolen goods than they are any apprenticeship qualification.

In order to prevent falls in prices, wages and profits, corporation laws have been implemented that restrain free competition. In Britain, anyone wishing to establish a corporation was required to obtain a charter from the king; it would appear that these charters were generally readily granted against payment of a fee. Towns were responsible for the inspection of all corporations within their jurisdiction, including the corporations' bye-laws. Towns were governed by traders and skilled workers, and it was in their interests to ensure the market for their own particular industry did not become saturated.

A town's inhabitants can easily join forces; even the most insignificant trades have been incorporated within a town. Trades employing only a few workers most readily form such unions: six wool-combers are necessary to keep a thousand spinners and weavers at work; by joining forces and thus eliminating the need for apprentices, they will have a monopoly over both the employment side and the manufacturing process, thus raising the price of their labor well above the average for their line of work.

The high duties imposed on foreign manufacturers and all goods imported by foreign merchants all serve the same purpose. Corporation laws enable people living in towns to raise their prices without having to worry about being undercut by free competition from their fellow countrymen. Further regulations also protect them against foreign competition.

Incorporation makes the act of the majority binding upon the whole. In free trade, this corporation can only be established with the unanimous consent of each trader, and only remains implemented for as long as each trader remains of the same mind. The majority of a corporation can enact bylaws, which limit competition more effectively and more sustainably than any voluntary combination.

Secondly, European policies, by increasing competition for some employments beyond what it naturally would be, cause inequality of an opposite kind.

Education and training in specific professions is considered important for the young, and private founders have established scholarships for this purpose, with the result that the numbers of people training in certain trades outnumber the jobs available. In Christian countries, the education of churchmen is paid for in this manner. The lengthy education required will not always result in a job, since many people are willing to work in a church voluntarily or accept a lower wage than such an education would otherwise have entitled them to; in this manner the competition of the poor takes away the reward of the rich.

In professions such as law and medicine, if an equal proportion of people were educated at the expense of the public, the competition would soon be so great that wages would drop. It might then not be worth self-aware father's while to pay for his son's education for either of these professions.

A teacher's salary is generally nowhere near as high as that of a lawyer or physician, because the teaching profession is crowded with disadvantaged people who have been educated at public expense to enter the church, whereas lawyers and physicians have funded their own education.

Thirdly, European policy, by obstructing the free circulation of labor and stock, both from employment to employment and from place to place, results in some cases in inequality in terms of the advantages and disadvantages offered by different jobs.

The statute of apprenticeship obstructs the free circulation of labor from one employment to another, even in the same place. Corporations' exclusive privileges obstruct circulation of labor from one place to another, even within the same trade. High wages are often paid to workmen in one business, while those in another business barely receive minimum wage. The tasks involved in certain trades are so similar that workers could easily exchange trades with one another if these absurd laws did not prevent it. The crafts of weaving plain linen and plain silk, for example, are almost entirely the same. That of weaving plain woolens is somewhat different—but the difference is so insignificant that a linen or silk weaver could easily be trained up within a few days.

Corporation laws hinder the free circulation of labor more than they do stock. It is much easier for a merchant to obtain authorization to trade in a town than it is for a poor tradesman to obtain work in it. In Britain after the destruction of the monasteries, it was enacted that every parish should be bound to provide for its own poor. When an independent workman carried his industry to a new parish, he was liable to be removed at the whim of the churchwarden.

# Chapter XI
## Of the Rent of Land

### Summary:

Rent is the price paid for the use of land. Landowners endeavor to leave tenants with the smallest amount of money for their subsistence.

A landlord will charge rent for the land based on the potential productivity of that land, so any improvements made to the land by the tenant in fact increase the rent, as if they had been made by the landlord.

The rent paid by the tenant for using the land is based on what the tenant can afford to pay, making it a monopoly.

Wages and profit are the causes of high or low price; high or low rent is the effect of it.

### Part I

Of the Produce of Land which always affords Rent

Food is always in demand. Land produces more than enough food to pay the tenant for his upkeep, with any remaining money being claimed by the landowner as rent. This rent goes up based on the land's productivity.

A land's rental cost varies according to its fertility and location. Rent will be higher for land located near town. A good transport infrastructure means that land in remote parts of the country is as accessible as that near major towns.

A moderately fertile cornfield produces a greater quantity of food than the best pasture. Corn is an annual crop, whereas livestock requires four or five years before it is ready to market. As an acre of land will produce a much smaller quantity of the one than of the other, this lower quantity must be compensated for by a higher price. In major towns, the demand for milk and hay for horses, together with the high price of butcher's meat, increase the value of grass.

The use of turnips, carrots, cabbages and other legumes to feed a greater number of cattle than when in grass will tend to reduce the price of butcher's meat over that of bread.

The landowner's rent in the case of a hop garden, fruit garden or vegetable garden will generally be higher, and the farmer's profit generally greater than for a corn or grass field. But to obtain the richness of soil needed for these crops costs more, so the landowner will charge a higher rent. On the other hand, the land requires more skillful management—hence the farmer will be paid a higher wage. In the past, productive vegetable gardens were the most productive in a farm.

The sugar colonies owned by European nations in the West Indies may be compared to vineyards. Their entire produce falls short of market demand from Europe, and can therefore be sold at high prices, covering the rent, profit and wages involved in preparing and bringing the produce to market. A sugar planter can expect rum and molasses to cover the costs for his cultivation, with his sugar being all clear profit.

Tobacco is the prime crop in Virginia and Maryland, and is more profitable than corn. Tobacco cultivation being prohibited throughout most of Europe means that Virginia and Maryland have a monopoly. Each worker on these tobacco plantations manages six thousand plants, which yield a thousand weight of tobacco, as well as four acres of Indian corn.

In Europe, corn (wheat) is the major crop, and a staple part of our diets. Except in particular situations, therefore, the rent of cornfields in Europe regulates the rent of all other cultivated land.

A rice field produces a much greater quantity of food than the most fertile cornfield, with an acre generally producing two crops a year. Though rice cultivation requires more labor, the resulting profit easily covers the cost. In Carolina, the cultivation of rice is found to be more profitable than that of corn, though their fields produce only one crop a year.

An acre of potatoes will produce three times the quantity of nourishment produced by the acre of wheat, and potatoes are cheaper to cultivate. As such, the same volume of land producing potatoes will provide for a much greater number of people than if it produced wheat.

# Part II

Of the Produce of Land, which sometimes does, and sometimes does not, afford Rent

The only produce which guarantees a profit to the farmer is food for human consumption. Other produce may or may not make a profit, depending on various circumstances.

After food, clothing and housing are the two basic human needs. Land provides more materials for clothing and construction than it does food. Productive land, however, may produce more food than clothing and construction materials, resulting in prices soaring for these materials. A surplus of produce results in price drops, whereas a scarcity results in price rises.

Many years ago, wool produced in Britain, which could neither be eaten nor used in construction, was sold to the wealthy, industrious country of Flanders, its price covering the rent of the land which produced it.

Rental fees for a good stone quarry in the London area would be high, contrary to the low fees in many parts of Scotland and Wales. Timber for construction is of great value in developed countries, with the result that rental for the forests producing it is expensive. But in many parts of North America, landowners are happy to have someone fell and remove their trees. Britain provides a market for the forests of Norway and the coasts of the Baltic—a market they could not find at home—thereby providing an income to their owners.

A country's population numbers are often aligned with the quantity of foodstuffs that country produces. When food is available, it is easy to find clothing and housing. When the labor of half of a society is sufficient to provide food for the entire society, the other half can be employed in providing products such as clothing and housing.

Food is not only the original source of rent, but other land-related produce, which goes towards paying rent, derives from improvements made in food production labor processes.

A mine is classed as fertile or barren, depending on the quantity of minerals it produces. The lowest price at which coal can be sold is the price which just covers replenishment of stock used to bring the coal to market, inclusive of its average profit.

The rental fee for land above ground is commonly a third of the gross produce, and is independent of the occasional variations in the crop. A rental contract of thirty years is considered a moderate period for land above ground, with ten years considered a good period for a coal mine. The tin mines of Cornwall, the most fertile in the world, bring in a rent of a sixth of their gross produce.

The demand for precious stones is high due to their scarcity, with demand driven by their beauty as ornaments rather than their utility. Consequently, wages and profit make up almost the whole of their high price.

Food not only constitutes the major share of the riches of the world, but it is the abundance of food which gives the principal part of their value to many other sorts of riches.

## Part III

Of the variations in the Proportion between the respective Values of that sort of Produce which always affords Rent, and of that which sometimes does, and sometimes does not, afford Rent

The increasing abundance of food, as a result of advances in agriculture and production processes, goes hand in hand with an increased demand for non-foodstuff agricultural produce, which is put to other uses, including decoration.

The demand for materials used in clothing and construction, useful materials of the land and precious metals is gradually increasing, with these items being exchanged for a greater quantity of food and hence for a higher price.

The value of a free-stone quarry will increase as the area immediately surrounding it develops, especially if it is the only one in the area. The market for the produce of a free-stone quarry is generally limited to the immediate surrounding region, with demand tending to be proportionate to the development and population of that small region.

The silver market is a worldwide commerce; unless global world finance improves, the demand for silver will not necessarily increase due to the improvement of even a large country in the neighborhood of the mine.

We should always bear in mind that labor is the real measure of the value of silver and all other commodities. In society, corn is produced through human industry, but the average produce of every type of industry is generally always in line with average consumption—the average supply to the average demand. At each stage of improvement, the production of equal quantities of corn requires equal quantities of labor, and as such, price. Steady improvement in production capacity and cultivation methods will be more or less counterbalanced by the steady price rise of cattle, the mainstay of farming.

This means that equal quantities of corn will, in every state of society, at every stage of improvement, be more representative of, or equivalent to, equal quantities of labor, than equal quantities of any other land-related produce. As such, corn is a more accurate measure of value than any other commodity or set of commodities. In all of these stages, therefore, corn is a better estimate of the real value of silver than any other commodity or set of commodities.

The quantity of precious metals in any country can increase due to abundance in its mines or increased produce of annual labor. The first of these causes is no doubt necessarily connected with a decrease in value of the precious metals, whereas the second is not.

In major towns, corn is always more expensive than in remote parts of the country. This, however, is the effect not of the real low price of silver, but of the real high price of corn. It does not require less labor to transport silver to a major town than to a remote part of the country; but it costs a great deal more to transport corn.

The civil war (in Britain) led to decreased tillage and commerce, resulting in a rise in corn prices. Another event was the bounty upon the export of corn, granted in 1688. The bounty, which encouraged tillage, led to greater abundance and consequently a drop in corn prices in the home market.

The value of silver has risen in proportion to that of corn during the course of the present century. In years of great scarcity, the bounty was suspended, though it definitely had an effect on prices throughout that period. Although resulting in extraordinary export during years of plenty, it would frequently have hindered the abundance of one year from compensating the scarcity of another.

The monetary price of labor in Britain has risen during the course of the present century. This seems to be due to increased demand for labor in Britain due to the country's prosperity, rather than to the drop in value of silver on the European market.

Since the discovery of America, the market for the produce of its silver mines has been growing increasingly extensive. America is itself a new market for the produce of its silver mines; its development in terms of agriculture, industry and population is much more rapid than that of the most thriving countries in Europe, so its demand is growing much more rapidly. The British colonies are a new market for silver, with an ever increasing demand for this precious metal, for both coinage and other purposes.

The sharp price rise for pigs and poultry in Britain was due mainly to the decrease in the numbers of people living in cottages and other small homes, since these more disadvantaged people often keep a few poultry or a sow and a few pigs. With fewer small-home dwellers, this type of commodity has become scarcer and hence the price has risen.

A farmer's cows produce more milk than will be used by their calves and the farmer's family, with most being produced during one season. But of all land produce, milk is perhaps the most perishable. In the summer months, when milk is most abundant, it will scarcely keep twenty-four hours. The farmer, by making it into fresh butter, is able to store a small part of it for nearly a week; by making it into salt butter, for a year; and by making it into cheese, he can store a large part of it for several years. Some of these stocks will be reserved for his family; the rest goes to market, to be sold at the best price he can get.

The rise in the nominal or monetary price of all these products is due not to a drop in the value of silver, but to a rise in their real price. Today they are worth a greater quantity of silver as well as a greater quantity of labor and subsistence than they were in the past; since it costs more in terms of labor and subsistence to bring them to market, they are worth more.

The market for butcher's meat is generally confined to the country in which it is produced. The market for wool and raw hides is improving. The quantity of fish brought to market is both limited and uncertain

Precious metals abound in countries with no mines, their quantity depending on the country's purchasing power. As with all luxury goods, this quantity is likely to rise during times of wealth and development in a country, and to fall during times of poverty and depression. Countries with an abundance of labor and provisions can afford to purchase more precious metals than their less-developed counterparts.

Effects of the Progress of Improvement upon the real Price of Manufactured Goods

As a business develops, with better machinery, higher levels of skill and specialization, the prices of its produce will drop considerably. Division of labor (specialization) and improvements in machinery can be carried out more extensively in base metals businesses than in any other.

## Conclusion of Chapter 11

Every improvement in a society raises the price of land rental. The extension of improvement and cultivation tends to raise it directly.

A rise in the price of produce raises the rent of land.

All improvements made to production capacity, which reduce the rent price of businesses, raise the rent of land.

Every increase in a society's real wealth tends indirectly to raise the real rent of land.

The entire annual produce of the land and labor of each country divides itself into three parts: the rent of land, the wages of labor, and the profits of stock. This profit provides a revenue to three different groups of people: the landowner (rent), the laborers (wages), and the farmer or entrepreneur (profit). These are the three great, original, and constituent orders of every civilized society, from whose revenue that of every other order is ultimately derived.

# Book II

Of The Nature, Accumulation, and Employment of Stock

## Introduction

Once division of labor has been implemented, the product of a man's own labor can provide for only a small part of his needs; the greater part is provided for by other men's labor, which he purchases with the produce of his own.

This purchase cannot be made until the produce of his labor has been sold.

A sufficient stock of provisions must be reserved in order to supply him with the materials and tools he needs for his work.

Labor can only be subdivided in proportion to the stock he has accumulated.

# Chapter I
## Of the Division of Stock

### Summary:

If a man's stock will not maintain him for more than a few days or weeks, he will consume it as sparingly as he can, while endeavoring to replace it, through labor, before it is all consumed. His revenue is in this case derived from his labor only. This is the situation for most of the working poor in all countries.

If, however, he has sufficient stock to maintain him for months or even years, he will endeavor to derive a revenue from the stock he does not need for his immediate consumption, reserving only the stock he needs until his revenue begins to come in.

His stock is divisible into two parts. The part he uses to derive a revenue is called his capital. The other covers his immediate consumption, and consists first of the portion of his whole stock originally reserved for this purpose; secondly, of his revenue; and thirdly, purchases such as clothes and furniture.

There are two ways in which capital may be employed to yield a profit. Firstly, it may be employed in raising, manufacturing or purchasing goods, which are then sold on at a profit. This is called circulating capital. Secondly, it can be invested in the improvement of land, the purchase of useful machines and trade tools. This is called fixed capital.

Different occupations require different proportions of fixed and circulating capital. A merchant's capital is circulating. A portion of the capital of every manufacturer will be fixed, in terms of the instruments of his trade; the greater part of the capital is circulated either in the wages of the workforce, or in purchase of materials, and is repaid by in price of the work.

The portion of a farmer's capital invested in agricultural material is fixed; the portion used for wages and the upkeep of his staff is circulating capital. Dairy cows that are not for sale but for milk production, are fixed capital; their maintenance is circulating capital.

# Chapter II
## Of Money, Considered as a Particular Branch of the General Stock of the Society, or of the Expense of Maintaining the National Capital.

### Summary:

The price of a product can be divided into three parts: one which pays the wages of labor, another the profits of stock, and a third the rent of land. The value of produce must resolve itself into the same three parts, divided among the inhabitants of the country in the form of wages of labor, profits of stock, or rent of land.

The gross rent of an estate consists of the amount paid by the farmer; the net rent is what is left over for the landlord after deducting expenses. His real wealth is in proportion not to his gross but net rent. The gross revenue of a country's inhabitants comprises the whole annual produce of their land and labor; the net revenue is what remains. Their real wealth is in proportion not to their gross but their net revenue.

The expense of maintaining fixed capital does not come from a society's net revenue. Fixed capital is used to increase productivity. Any streamlining improvements to production processes and workforce are viewed as beneficial to a society. The expense of maintaining a large country's fixed capital may be compared to the expense of repairs made to a private estate.

Money is the only part of a society's circulating capital, and its maintenance can result in a decrease in neat revenue. Fixed capital, and that part of circulating capital which consists of money, are similar.

The amount of money circulating in a particular country incurs expense in terms of its collection and replenishment; both expenses are deducted from a society's net revenue. A quantity of gold and silver, and of labor, instead of increasing the stock reserved for immediate consumption, is used to maintain commercial tool.

When we talk of a particular sum of money, we are referring to physical money. But when we say that a man is worth a hundred pounds a year, we mean not only his annual wage, but the value of the goods he is able to purchase annually.

Though a country's inhabitants may receive monetary wages, their real revenue is measured in terms of the quantity of consumable goods they can purchase.

This is even more the case for a society. As money changes hands repeatedly, it can never be equal to the revenue of all of a society's members; so the amount of money circulating in a country must always be of less value than the annual sum paid using it.

Machinery, which represents fixed capital, forms the monetary part of circulating capital: savings made in purchasing and maintaining these machines increases net revenue, so savings in terms of collecting and replenishing the monetary part of circulating capital is an improvement of the same kind.

Replacing gold and silver with banknotes replaces a very expensive tool of trade with a less costly one, making circulation less expensive to implement and maintain.

When people trust a banker implicitly in terms of lending promissory notes, these notes will have the same value as gold and silver. Such a banker can grant loans to his customers, of his own promissory notes; for example, for an amount of a hundred thousand pounds. His customers pay him the same interest as if he had lent them money; this interest will be his profit. Though he generally has notes in circulation of up to a hundred thousand pounds, amounts of twenty thousand pounds in gold and silver often suffice for occasional demands. If different operations of the same kind are carried out simultaneously by many different banks and bankers, the entire circulation may be conducted with only a fifth of the gold and silver which would otherwise have been required.

For example, say the entire circulating money of a particular country amounts to one million sterling; let us suppose that bankers issue promissory notes for an amount of one million, reserving two hundred thousand pounds for occasional requests; there would be eight hundred thousand pounds in gold and silver, and a million bank notes, or eighteen hundred thousand pounds of banknotes and money in circulation. But the annual produce of the land and labor of the country had before required only one million to circulate. This means there is an excess of eight hundred thousand pounds over and above what can be circulated in the country. This money cannot be absorbed by the country's economy and will therefore be sent abroad to a market that can employ it. Banknotes cannot go abroad since it cannot be used far from its issuing bank, so gold and silver, to the amount of eight hundred thousand pounds, will be sent abroad.

If they employ it in purchasing foreign goods for home consumption, they may purchase unproductive goods such as wines, or they may purchase materials, tools and provisions to employ and maintain additional workforce.

Three things are required in order to establish an industry: materials to work on, tools to work with, and wages to pay for the labor involved. Money is neither a material to work on, nor a tool to work with, and though a worker's wages are commonly paid to him in money, his real revenue consists not of the money but the money's worth; i.e., not in the physical metal coins but in what he can buy for them.

Many years ago, Scotland saw the establishment of some of the first banking companies in almost every town. The effects of this were those described above. The country's business is almost entirely carried out using the banknotes issued by various banking companies, for purchases and payments of all kinds. Silver and gold are used only rarely. Although the performance of these various companies has not been exceptionable, and required an act of parliament to regulate it, the country derived great benefit from their trade. Trade in Glasgow doubled within fifteen years of the establishment of the first banks there, and in Scotland it more than quadrupled since the establishment of the first two public banks in Edinburgh, of which the one, the Bank of Scotland, was established by act of parliament in 1695, and the other, Royal Bank, by royal charter in 1727.

The amount of banknotes circulating in a particular country should never exceed the amount of gold and silver that country possesses. Should this occur, there would be a run on the banks for these superfluous banknotes, and if they showed any problems in terms of payment, the alarm would necessarily increase the run.

The Bank of Britain is the main circulating bank in Europe. Incorporated through an act of parliament, by charter dated 27 July 1694, it at that time advanced a sum to the newly established government of £1,200,000 for an annuity of £100,000, or for £96,000 a year, at an eight percent interest rate, and £4,000 a year to cover management expenses. We can assume that the new government's credit must have been very low for it to have been obliged to borrow at such a high interest rate.

The stability of the bank of Britain is equal to that of the British Government. All that it has advanced to the public must be lost before its creditors can sustain any loss. No other banking corporation in Britain can be established through an act of parliament or can consist of more than six members. It acts not only as an ordinary bank but as a great engine of state. It receives and pays the greater part of the annuities due to public creditors; it circulates exchequer bills; and it advances an annual amount to the government to cover land and malt taxes, which are frequently not reimbursed before several years. Due to these various operations, it may, at no fault of its directors, sometimes overstock in terms of the amount of banknotes in circulation.

A country's monetary circulation can be divided into two types: that from one dealer to another; and that between dealers and consumers. Although the same pieces of money, whether notes or metal, may be employed in both of these circulations, since both are constantly ongoing simultaneously, each requires a certain stock of money, of one kind or another, in order to carry it out. The value of the goods circulated between the various dealers should never exceed the value of those circulated between dealers and consumers; whatever is bought by dealers is ultimately sold to consumers. Circulation between dealers, which is carried out wholesale, requires a relatively large stock of money; whereas between dealers and consumers, which generally involves retail, requires a relatively small stock.

In the currencies of North America, banknotes were used for sums as small as a shilling, and formed the bulk of the entire circulation. It is preferable not to issue bank notes for a value of under £5; as such, banknotes would probably be confined to circulation between dealers, as is the case currently in London where no bank notes are issued for a value of under £10.

Where banknotes is pretty much confined to circulation between dealers, as is the case in London, there is always plenty of gold and silver. Where banknotes is also used for much of the circulation between dealers and consumers, as is the case in Scotland and even more so in North America, gold and silver are practically not used at all in the country, with almost all ordinary transactions being carried out in banknotes.

The paper currencies of North America consisted not of bank notes payable to the bearer on demand but of a government paper, of which payment was not guaranteed until several years after its issue; and though the colony governments paid no interest to the holders of this paper, they made it legal tender of payment for the full value for which it was issued.

Indeed, the Government of Pennsylvania, when they first issued banknotes in 1722, pretended to render their paper of equal value with gold and silver, by enacting penalties against all those who made any difference between the price of their goods when selling them for a colony paper as opposed to for gold and silver.

# Chapter III
## Of the Accumulation of Capital, or of Productive and Unproductive Labor.

### Summary:

Productive labor adds value to its subject; unproductive labor does not. A manufacturer adds value to the materials he works on. A house servant adds nothing. Although the manufacturer receives wages from his boss, he is actually maintained by his boss at no real cost since the value of his wages is covered, including a profit, by the value he has added to the subject on which he has worked.

The labor of some jobs, such as house servant, is unproductive of any permanent value in a society. The sovereign, with all the officers of justice and war who serve under him, and the whole army and navy, are unproductive workers. The protection, security and defense of the commonwealth do not generate a profit enabling the purchase this protection, security and defense the following year. Some professions involving unproductive labor are churchmen, lawyers, physicians, actors and musicians. None of these are productive laborers.

Productive and unproductive laborers, as well as the unemployed, are all maintained by the annual produce of the land and labor of the country. This produce must have certain limits.

The produce of the land, whether farmed or manufactured by productive laborers, can be divided into two parts. The first, the produce of the land, is used to replace the farmer's capital; the second pays his profit and the rent of the landowner, and thus provides a revenue both to the owner of the capital, as the profits of his stock, and to the person who owns the productive land, in the form of rent. In the case of a large business, the largest part goes towards replacing the capital of entrepreneur; the other pays his profit, and thus constitutes a revenue to the person who owns the capital.

If his wages permit it, even a common laborer can hire a house servant, or perhaps spend his wages on entertainment, such as a theatre show; in this way, he contributes a share towards maintaining unproductive labor. Or he may pay taxes, thus contributing towards maintaining more useful, but equally unproductive, labor.

The proportion between capital and revenue regulates the proportion between industry and idleness. Wherever capital predominates, industry prevails; wherever revenue predominates, idleness prevails.

Capital is increased by frugality, and diminished by extravagance. Whatever a person saves from his revenue, he adds to his capital, and either employs it himself in hiring additional productive laborers, or enables another person to do so by lending it to him at interest, thus making a profit. As a person's capital can be increased only by what he saves from his annual revenue or profit, likewise a society's capital can be increased only in the same manner. Frugality, and not industry, is the immediate cause of the increase of capital. Industry, indeed, provides the subject which frugality accumulates; but whatever industry might acquire, if not saved up and stored through frugality, the capital would not grow.

What a frugal man saves annually can be used to hire additional productive laborers for the following year, but doing so means he will have to maintain this number of laborers in the years to come. If the extravagant spending of some were not compensated by the frugality of others, the extravagant spenders sponging off the industrious would lead to the country's impoverishment.

However we view the real wealth and revenue of a country, prodigal spenders can be seen as the public enemy, and frugal people as public benefactors. Imprudent and unsuccessful projects in agriculture, mining, fishing, trade and manufacturing also tend to diminish the funds destined for the maintenance of productive labor.

Great nations are sometimes impoverished by public extravagance and misconduct; almost the entire public revenue is employed in maintaining unproductive labor; lawyers, churchmen, army and navy generals, who in time of peace produce nothing and in time of war acquire nothing which can compensate for the expense of maintaining them. Such people are all maintained, therefore, by the produce of other men's labor.

The expense involved in leisure events such as festivals, where commodities are provided for a greater amount of people than those employed at the event, often result in as much as half of these commodities being thrown out afterwards, resulting in huge amounts of waste. If the expense invested in this entertainment had been put towards setting up a business of masons, carpenters, upholsterers, mechanics, etc., for example, a quantity of provisions of equal value would have been distributed among a still greater number of people, who would have bought them in monetary weight and not lost or thrown away a single ounce of them.

# Chapter IV
## Of Stock Lent at Interest

## Summary:

Stock lent at interest always represents capital for the lender. He expects it to be repaid in due course. In the meantime, the borrower pays him a certain annual fee for the use of it. The borrower can use it either as capital or for immediate consumption. If he uses it as capital, he will be investing in productive labor that will make him a profit. If he uses it for immediate consumption, he is contributing toward the idle what was destined to support the industrious.

Almost all interest-based loans are made in money—either banknotes, gold or silver; however, what the borrower really wants and what the lender provides is not the actual money but the money's worth, or the goods it can purchase. By granting a loan, a lender is in effect assigning the borrower the right to a certain portion of the annual produce of the land and labor of the country, to be used as the borrower pleases.

In some countries, interest on money lending has been prohibited by law. Rather than preventing problems, this regulation has in fact increased them since the debtor is obliged to pay not only for the use of the money but for the risk his creditor runs, by accepting compensation for that use.

In countries where interest is permitted, the law to prevent extortion generally fixes the highest rate possible without incurring a penalty. In Britain, where money is lent to the government at a 3% interest rate and to private people at 4%, the present legal rate of 5% is the accepted norm.

The ordinary market price of land depends upon the ordinary market interest rate. A person who has capital from which he wishes to derive a revenue without taking the trouble to employ it himself may decide to invest it in land or lend it out at interest.

# Chapter V
## Of the Different Employments of Capitals

## Summary:
Though all capital is destined for the maintenance of productive labor, the quantity of labor that can be employed for a specific amount of capital will vary depending on the type of employment, in the same way the value that employment adds to the annual produce of the land and the labor of the country.

Capital may be employed in four different ways:

procuring the crude products required for a society's use and consumption;

manufacturing and preparing those products for consumption;

transporting the crude or manufactured products from their places of origin to those where they are wanted;

dividing particular portions of either into smaller portions to suit occasional demands from those who want them.

The capital of the retailer replaces, together with its profits, that of the merchant from whom he purchases goods, thereby enabling him to continue his business.

The capital of the wholesale merchant replaces, together with their profits, the capitals of the farmers and manufacturers from whom he purchases the crude and manufactured produce he deals in, thereby enabling them to continue their respective trades.

Part of the capital of the master manufacturer is employed as fixed capital in the instruments of his trade and replaces, together with its profits, that of the craftsmen from whom he purchases them. Part of his circulating capital is employed in purchasing materials and replaces, with their profits, the capitals of the farmers and miners from whom he purchases them. But a great part of it is distributed among the workmen he employs.

Capital invested in agriculture not only enables a greater quantity of productive labor than the same amount of capital employed in manufacturing, but adds much greater value to the annual produce of the land and labor of the country and to the real wealth and revenue of its inhabitants. Of all the ways in which capital can be employed, this is by far the most advantageous to society.

The revenue of all the inhabitants of a country will be in proportion to the value of the annual produce of their land and labor. The activity that adds the greatest value to annual produce is agriculture—as demonstrated by the rapid growth in wealth of American colonies, which focus primarily on agriculture. They have no manufacturing businesses, with the exception of private family-run household businesses managed by women and children. The greater part of America's export and coastal trade is conducted with the capital of merchants located in Britain. Even the retail stores and warehouses in some provinces, notably Virginia and Maryland, belong to UK merchants.

All forms of wholesale trade can be categorized into three types:

Home trade, involving internal purchase and sale of produce of industries within that country.

Foreign trade, involving the purchase of foreign goods for home consumption.

Carrying trade, involving transactions of commerce of foreign countries, or trade of surplus produce from one country to another.

When an industry's produce exceeds demand, the surplus must be marketed abroad, in exchange for something for which there is a demand. The land and labor of Britain generally produce more than the demand of the home market requires; the surplus is therefore marketed abroad, in exchange for something for which there is a demand at home. About 96,000 hogsheads of tobacco are purchased annually in Virginia and Maryland with part of the surplus produce of British industry, but Britain does not require more than 14,000; if the remaining 82,000 cannot be exported and sold in exchange for something more in demand at home, importation of these products must cease, and with it the productive labor of all the inhabitants of Britain currently employed in preparing the goods with which these 82,000 hogsheads are purchased annually.

# Book III

Of the Different Progress of Opulence in Different Nations

## Chapter I
### Of the Natural Progress of Opulence

### Summary:

Commerce, in any civilized society, consists of the exchange of crude produce for manufactured goods. The countryside supplies the town with crude materials for manufacture; in turn, inhabitants of the countryside purchase manufactured goods from the town.

The capital of every growing society is primarily employed in agriculture, then in manufacturing businesses, and lastly in foreign trade. Men choose to invest their capital in the cultivation of land rather than manufacturing or foreign trade. Investments in land offer more security than investments in trade.

Cultivating land requires skilled tradesmen. Town and country inhabitants are mutually beneficial to each other, with the town providing a market for the country folk to sell their produce in exchange for the town's manufactured goods. The quantity of manufactured goods a town sells to the country regulates the quantity of raw materials they buy.

# Chapter II
## Of the Discouragement of Agriculture in the Ancient State of Europe, After the Fall of the Roman Empire

### Summary:

When the German nations overran the western provinces of the Roman Empire, turmoil reigned for several centuries, with towns largely deserted and the countryside left uncultivated. During this time, the chiefs and leaders of those nations acquired or usurped to themselves the greater part of this mostly uncultivated land. The result was that all of this land ended up being by various proprietors.

Land represented not only a means of subsistence, but was a sign of power and protection. As such, it was felt that it was preferable not to divide land up, but rather to keep it within a family. This resulted in the introduction of the law of primogeniture, under which land passed to the eldest son of a family—the origin of the right of succession.

Entails were the natural consequences of the law of primogeniture. Introduced to limit the inheritance of property to certain heirs over a number of generations, they prevented land being passed outside the family by gift or folly, or by the misfortune of any of its successive owners. In the case of, for example, a principality, entails are indeed useful as they could well ensure the welfare of perhaps thousands of people against the caprice or extravagance of one man. But in Europe, nothing could be more absurd. Entails are used as a means of maintaining the exclusive privileges of nobility; in Scotland, more than a third of the land is under strict entail. Great landlords, however, are rarely great improvers of the land, preferring to invest their annual savings in new purchases rather than in the improvement of their old estate.

Man generally prefers to hire serfs rather than skilled laborers. Although sugar and tobacco plantations provide sufficient profit to pay for the upkeep of slaves, corn plantations do not. In the English colonies, of which the principal produce is corn, work is carried out by laborers. The resolution of the Quakers in Pennsylvania to free all their Negro slaves suggests that slaves were not widely used on the land there. The work on our sugar colonies is carried out entirely by slaves, and on our tobacco plantations a large part of it. Profits from sugar plantations are greater than for any other cultivation in Europe or America. Profits from tobacco plantations are superior to those of corn. This explains the fact that there are more Negro slaves than whites working in our sugar plantations than tobacco plantations.

# Chapter III
## Of the Rise and Progress of Cities and Towns, After the Fall of the Roman Empire

## Summary:

After the fall of the Roman Empire, landowners lived in fortified castles on their own estates; towns were chiefly inhabited by tradesmen and mechanics, in more or less the same servile conditions as the peasants.

But despite these conditions, the inhabitants of towns had more freedom than their country-dwelling counterparts. The kings of a particular country derived revenue from poll taxes charged for land rented out as farmland (sub-contracted) for a fee; the townspeople, or burghers, frequently got to farm the revenues which arose out of their own town. At first, the farmland was rented out to the burghers for a specific number of years; over time, however, it became standard practice to rent it to them in perpetuity. This was the origin of a free burgh, free burghers or free traders, when the burghers established corporations, with their own laws, town councils and government, and built walls for their security, which they defended against attack.

In those days, no sovereign was able to protect his weaker subjects from the oppression of the great lords. The lords despised the burghers due to their wealth, and plunders were frequent. The burghers hated and feared the lords, as did the king. This resulted in the burghers and king mutually supporting each other against the lords. It was in the king's interest to ensure the burghers were as secure and independent of the lords as possible. He therefore granted the burghers their own magistrates, and the privilege of making bylaws for their own government, as well as the right to build walls for their defense. He also introduced a form of military discipline for them. As such, he gave them all the means of security and independence it was in his power to bestow.

In Britain, the cities became so strong that the sovereign could not impose a tax on them (besides the abovementioned farm rent) without their consent. They were often asked to send deputies to the kingdom's general assembly, where they sometimes joined with clergy and barons to grant extraordinary aid to the king. Being more favorable to his power, these deputies seem to have been employed by the king as a counterbalance at these assemblies, against the authority of the great lords.

As a result, order and good government was established in the cities, together with liberty and security for the inhabitants—while in the country, people were exposed to violence and chaos.

# Chapter IV
## How the Commerce of Towns Contributed to the Improvement of the Country

## Summary:

The growth and increasing wealth of commercial and manufacturing towns contributed to the improvement and cultivation of the countries to which they belonged in three different ways:

Firstly, by providing a large market for the country's crude produce, they encouraged its further cultivation and improvement.

Secondly, the wealth acquired by the city inhabitants was frequently used to purchase land. Merchants, keen to become country gentlemen, were more likely to improve the land they purchased. Such merchants saw a return on their investment and were not afraid to invest capital in improving their land, as they realized it would increase its value.

Thirdly, commerce and manufacturing gradually introduced order and good government amongst a country's inhabitants, in contrast to their previous existence, which involved ongoing wars with their neighbors and servile dependency upon their superiors. This is viewed as being the most important change brought about by towns' growth.

Merchants, however, were unaware of the revolution their industry was gradually bringing about, acting merely in their own interests in pursuit of making money wherever they could. Throughout most of Europe, commerce and manufacturing in cities led to improvements in the countryside.

Growth rates in European countries, whose wealth depends on commerce, is slow compared to that in the North American colonies, whose wealth depends on agriculture. In terms of population growth, population doubles in Europe only every five hundred years or so, whereas in North America it doubles every twenty years.

The law of primogeniture in Europe prevents the division of great estates, thus hindering the multiplication of small landlords. The same regulations keep so much land out of the market that land which is sold is at a monopoly price. The result is that very little capital is invested in cultivation and improvement of land.

In North America, on the contrary, fifty to sixty pounds will generally buy enough stock to begin a plantation. The purchase and improvement of uncultivated land there is the most profitable investment for both small and large amounts of capital, and the fastest road to wealth. Such land is very cheap in North America, going for prices way below the value of the natural produce—which is not the case in Europe, or indeed in any country where the land is all privately owned.

If estates were divided equally among all of the children upon the death of a proprietor with a numerous family, the estate would generally be sold, with the result that so much land would come to market that it could no longer sell at a monopoly price. As such, a small amount of capital invested in purchasing land would be as attractive an investment opportunity as any.

The people occupying land were dependent on both the great landlord and his servants. The rent paid by both tenants renting under the feudal system and tenants at will was nowhere near equivalent to the subsistence the land provided them. A crown, half a crown, a sheep or a lamb was a common means of rent some years ago in the Highlands of Scotland for lands which maintained a family. This is still the case in some places today. In a country where the surplus produce of a large estate must be consumed upon the estate itself, it is often more convenient for the landlord if part of it is consumed at a distance from his house, provided those consuming it are dependent upon him. He is thereby saved from the embarrassment of either too large a company or too large a family. A tenant at will who has sufficient land to maintain his family for little more than a quit-rent is as dependent upon the landlord as any servant. Such a landlord provides food for his servants at his own home, and feeds his tenants at their houses. Their subsistence is therefore derived from his bounty, and depends upon his goodwill.

Wealth resided in the great landlords, and with it, power over their tenants and servants. They became both judges and leaders for those living on their estates. They maintained order and enforced laws within their respective estates by mobilizing the inhabitants against injustices committed by an individual. No other person, including the king, had sufficient authority to do this; in these ancient times, the king was little more than the greatest landlord of his dominions, and was respected by the great landlords mainly in terms of ensuring mutual defense against common enemies. For the king to have enforced payment of a small debt within the lands of a great landlord, in which all the inhabitants were armed and stood by one another, would have been akin to him ending a civil war. The king therefore left the administration of justice throughout most of the country to those capable of administering it, and left the command of the militia to those whom that militia would obey.

These territorial jurisdictions did not, however, originate from the feudal system. Not only the highest jurisdictions, both civil and criminal, but the power of levying troops, of coinage, and even that of making bylaws for the government of their own people were all the absolute right of the great landlords several centuries before feudal law was first introduced in Europe. The authority and jurisdiction of the Saxon lords in Britain appear to have been just as strong before the Conquest as that of any of the Norman lords after it—yet the feudal system is believed to have become common law in Britain only after the Conquest. There is also substantial evidence that the lords in France held absolute ownership of estates long before the feudal law was introduced in that country. This authority and jurisdiction came from ownership of an estate. There is historical proof of this even later than the times of the French and English monarchies. Only thirty years ago, Mr. Cameron of Lochiel from Lochaber in Scotland, a landholder by feudal tenure under the Duke of Argyll, was neither a noble nor a tenant in chief, yet exercised the highest criminal jurisdictions over his own people, despite having no legal right to do so. He is said to have done so fairly, though without any of the formalities of justice. Probably the state of that part of the country at that time made it necessary for him to assume this authority in order to maintain public peace. In 1745, Mr. Cameron, whose rent never exceeded £500 a year, mobilized 800 of his own people into rebellion with him.

The introduction of the feudal system may be viewed as an attempt to moderate the authority of the great allodial lords. It established subordination, from the king down to the smallest landlord. Under this system, the rent and management of a landlord's land was controlled by his immediate superior, and that of the great landlords was controlled by the king, who was charged with the maintenance and education of the pupil, and who, from his authority as guardian, had the right to arrange marriage, provided it was not deemed unsuitable to the pupil's rank. This system strengthened the authority of the king and weakened that of the great landlords; however, it did not result in order and good government amongst country dwellers. Government authority remained weak at the top and strong amongst the lower ranks, and the feudal system did not enable the king to prevent violence amongst the great lords. They continued to fight amongst each other at will almost continually, as well as against the king, and the countryside remained a place of violence, rapine and disorder.

But it was not the violence that reigned under the feudal system that brought about the growth and progression of society; it was foreign trade and industry, which gradually provided the great landlords with something for which they could exchange the whole surplus produce of their lands and which they could consume themselves, without sharing it either with tenants or servants. Self-interest above the interests of others seems to have been the vile maxim of the masters of mankind, throughout the ages. The wealthy would sooner spend their money on themselves than invest it in renting land to others. They would happily purchase a pair of diamond buckles or some other frivolous and useless item for an amount that would have maintained 1000 men for a year. The thinking behind this was that the frivolous purchase was all their own, whereas by renting their land out, they would have been sharing with 1000 other people. This wealth eroded over time, however, as the great landowners could not maintain this extravagant lifestyle.

In a country where there is no foreign trade or major manufacturing businesses, a man earning £10,000 a year cannot employ his revenue in any other way than maintaining perhaps 1000 families, all of whom work for him. In the present state of Europe, a man earning £10,000 a year can spend his whole revenue—and generally does so—without directly maintaining as few as twenty people or employing just ten of even the most menial servants. Indirectly, however, he is probably maintaining as many or even more people than he could have done if renting out his land to these people because, although the quantity of precious items he purchases with his revenue is very small, the number of workmen employed in manufacturing them is great. The high price of the frivolous item reflects the wages of their labor and the profits of all their immediate employers. By paying this steep price, he is indirectly paying all these wages and profits, and thus indirectly contributing to the maintenance of all the workmen and their employers. In terms of their annual maintenance, however, he is contributing a very small portion. Though he contributes toward their maintenance, they are all more or less independent of him since they can generally all be maintained without him.

When great landlords spend their rents in maintaining their tenants and servants, each maintains his own tenants and servants. But when these landlords spend their rents maintaining tradesmen and skilled workers, they may in fact, as a whole, be maintaining as many or more people than before, on account of the waste incurred when providing hospitality. Each landlord individually, however, contributes only a very small share to the maintenance of each individual of this greater number. Each tradesman or skilled worker derives his subsistence from the employment not of one but of a hundred or a thousand different customers. Though in some measure obliged to them all, therefore, he is not absolutely dependent upon any individual one of them.

As a result, the great landlords' personal expenses gradually increased and the number of servants they hired decreased, until they could no longer hire any at all. They also started to find themselves having to dismiss their tenants. Farms were enlarged and the number of tenants reduced to just the necessary amount needed to cultivate the land. By reducing these unnecessary mouths and by exploiting the farm to its full potential, the landlord obtained a greater surplus and hence profit, which he was able to spend on himself, purchasing from merchants and manufacturers, in the same way he done in the past. The landowner would often then be tempted to increase the rent for his land, usually above what it was actually worth. His tenants would agree to this, on the condition that they could rent the land for a specified number of years, thus guaranteeing them the income required to recover whatever they invested in the further improvement of the land. The landlords, keen to maintain their extravagant lifestyles, agreed to this—hence the origin of the long-term lease.

A tenant at will who pays the full value of the land is not totally dependent upon the landlord. The financial benefits they receive from one another are mutual and equal, and the tenant is risking neither life nor fortune by working for the landlord. If, on the other hand, he has a long-term lease, he is totally independent; his landlord cannot expect any service of him beyond what is expressly stipulated in the lease or imposed upon him by the country's laws.

With tenants now having become independent and the servants being dismissed, the great landlords no longer had any power to become involved in the country's legal or peace-related matters. Having sold their birthright—not like Esau, for a mess of pottage at a time of hunger and necessity, but through extravagance, for trinkets and baubles—they became as insignificant as any common burgher or tradesman in a city. Regular governments were established in both the countryside and the cities, and no one had the power to disrupt their operation.

As an aside, I feel it is relevant to point out here that in commercial countries, there are very few old land-owning families; i.e., that have passed estates from father to son for many successive generations. In countries in which there is little commerce, however, such as Wales or the Highlands of Scotland, there are many such families. Arabian history books are full of genealogies, and the history book written by Tartar Khan, which has been translated into several European languages, contains proof that ancient families are very common among such nations. In countries where a wealthy man's revenue is spent solely on maintaining as many people as possible, he is unlikely to live beyond his means. But where he can spend his revenue on himself, he tends to have no limitations to his expenditure, which is driven by self-interest. In commercial countries, therefore, riches, in spite of laws implemented with a view to preventing their dissipation, very seldom remain long in the same family. Among simple nations, on the contrary, they frequently do, without the existence of any such laws. Among nations of shepherds such as the Tartars and Arabs, for example, the consumable nature of their property renders all such regulations impossible.

Consequently, a major revolution in terms of public happiness was brought about by two different classes of people, neither of which had the public's interests at heart. Great landlords were driven by self-interest and extravagance. Merchants and industrialists, much less frivolous, acted with a view to self-sustenance, striving to make money wherever possible. Neither had the knowledge or foresight of the great revolution which the folly of the one and the industry of the other were gradually bringing about.

Indeed, throughout the greater part of Europe, trade and industry in cities, rather than being the *result* of a country's improvement and growth, have been the driving force behind it.

This situation, however, being contrary to the natural course of things, is both slow and uncertain. Compare the slow progress of the European countries, whose wealth depends on commerce and manufacturing, with the rapid progress of the North American colonies, whose wealth depends entirely on agriculture. Throughout most of Europe, population doubles only every five hundred years or so; in the North American colonies, it doubles about every twenty years.

The law of primogeniture in Europe prevents the division of great estates, thereby hindering the multiplication of small landlords. A small landlord, however, who knows every part of his little territory, will take a certain pride in it and will enjoy not only cultivating but embellishing it— with the result that he will be one of the best, most industrious, intelligent and successful landowners. Furthermore, these same regulations keep so much land out of the market that there is always more capital to buy than there is land to sell, so what is sold always sells at a monopoly price. Rent never pays the interest of the purchase fee, nor does it cover repairs and other occasional charges.

Throughout Europe, investing a small amount of capital in land is an unprofitable investment. A middle-class man may, upon retirement, decide to invest his small amount of capital in land, for the security this provides. A professional man may also secure his savings in the same way. But a young man who, instead of working as a tradesman or in some other profession, invests two or three thousand pounds in the purchase and cultivation of a small piece of land can live very happily and independently—although forgoing the fortune he may have made had he invested otherwise. The latter may well become a farmer, though the small quantity of land, coupled with the high price often means that there will not be a great amount to spare to invest in the land's cultivation and improvement.

In North America, on the contrary, fifty to sixty pounds is generally sufficient to begin a plantation. The purchase and improvement of uncultivated land there is the most profitable investment for both small and large amounts of capital, and the fastest road to wealth. This land in North America goes for next to nothing, at prices way below the value of the natural produce—which is not the case in Europe, or indeed in any country where the land is all privately owned. If estates were divided equally among all of the children upon the death of a landlord with a numerous family, the estate would generally be sold, with the result that so much land would come to market that it could no longer sell at a monopoly price. As such, the free rent of the land would come closer to covering the interest of the purchase price, and a small amount of capital invested in purchasing land would be as profitable an investment as any other.

# Book IV

Of Systems of Political Economy

Political economy proposes to enrich both the people and the sovereign.

# Chapter I
## Of the Principle of the Commercial or Mercantile System

### Summary:

The popular notion that wealth means money (gold and silver) arises from the fact that money is used both as an instrument of commerce and as a measure of value, in the sense that if we have money, we can readily obtain whatever we need.

A rich country abounds in money. A nation's consumable goods, on the other hand, may exist in abundance one year and be lacking the next year, due to waste and extravagance.

The governments of Spain and Portugal, the principal exporters of gold and silver throughout Europe, prohibited the export of gold and silver. When these two countries became commercial, merchants found this prohibition to be damaging to trade. They argued that export of these precious metals could only be prevented by addressing the balance of trade: when a country exports a greater value than it imports, a balance is owed by the foreign nations, which is paid in gold and silver, thereby increasing the quantity of these precious metals in the kingdom. On the other hand, when a country imports a greater value than it exports, a balance is owed to the foreign nations, which when paid will diminish the quantity of these precious metals in the kingdom. Furthermore, government prohibition was unable to hinder the exportation of gold and silver since it is easily smuggled.

Government attention was also focused on another, equally fruitless, notion. Home industry and trade, which creates many jobs, was viewed as secondary to foreign trade, since it neither brought money into a country nor sent any out, and as such it was felt that home trade would not increase a country's wealth.

A country that has the means to buy gold and silver will never have a shortage of these precious metals. The quantity of commodities purchased or produced is always regulated by market demand. But no commodities are more easily regulated by this demand than gold and silver, since its small size and high value mean it is easily transported from one place to another—from a place where it is cheap to a market where it is expensive. The ease with which gold and silver can be transported from locations in which it is plentiful to those in which it is in high demand mean that their price does not fluctuate continually, as is the case with most other commodities.

When money is scarce, traders will barter, though this is not without its inconveniences. Buying and selling on credit is more secure—but the best situation is always a well-regulated supply of money. A lack of money in a country does not necessarily mean a lack of gold and silver pieces in circulation, but rather that many people want those pieces but have nothing to give for them. It is not a lack of gold and silver, but rather the problems people face trying to get loans or reimbursing those loans that lead to complaints about lack of money.

Wealth is not represented by money, gold or silver, but rather what money can purchase, and as such is valuable only for purchasing. Money constitutes part of the national capital, but generally only a small—and the most unprofitable—part. Wealth is not constituted by money, but money is the established instrument of commerce, used to obtain commodities or labor. Furthermore, most commodities are more perishable than money and therefore frequently incur losses. A merchant's capital sometimes consists entirely of perishable goods intended for trade against money.

Goods can serve many other purposes besides being traded for money, but money can serve no other purpose besides purchasing goods. Men do not desire money for money's sake, but for what they can purchase with it.

Importing gold and silver is not the sole benefit a nation derives from its foreign trade. Foreign trade also moves out the surplus part of a country's produce for which there is no demand at home, and brings back something else for which there is a demand. Foreign trade also extends the home market, which enables the division of labor to be carried out to the highest perfection. Broadening the market encourages the country to improve its productive power and to increase its annual produce, thus growing its real revenue and wealth.

In light of this belief that wealth was constituted by gold and silver, and that only balance of trade could bring these into a country which lacked mines, many governments felt it made sense economically to restrain the importation of foreign goods and to increase the exportation of domestic produce. These restraints on foreign imports were placed on goods that could be produced at home, and especially on goods imported from countries with which trade was thought to be disadvantageous. The restraints included high duties and in some cases total prohibition.

Exportation was encouraged through a number of measures including bounties, trade agreements with foreign states, and the establishment of colonies. Bounties encouraged start-up businesses and specialized industries. Under the trade agreements, the country would be granted specific privileges by a foreign state for its commodities. The establishment of colonies created a monopoly of the market for the merchants of the country which established them.

# Chapter II
## Of Restraints upon Importation from Foreign Countries of Such Goods as can be Produced at Home

## Summary:

Placing restrictions on the importation of foreign goods produced at home creates a monopoly for the home market, hence benefitting the producers of these goods; for example, the ban on the import of live cattle gave Britain's cattle farmers the monopoly of the home market for butcher's meat; the high duty on importing corn amounts to a prohibition.

Although this monopoly ensures the country a greater share of labor and stock, whether it benefits the society's industry as a whole is uncertain. Regulation of a society's commerce cannot increase the quantity of industry beyond what its capital can maintain. It can only divert a portion of the country's industry into a direction into which it might not otherwise have gone, which will not necessarily be more advantageous to the society than if it had been left unregulated.

Most people endeavor to employ their capital as near to their home market as possible. It is only with a view to making a profit that an individual employs his capital in support of industry, and he will always endeavor to direct that industry so that its produce will be of the greatest possible value. Driven by self-interest and the advantages he can gain from his capital, a man invests in domestic rather than foreign industry, and as such is unintentionally investing in the market that is most advantageous to society.

Imposing a regulation which creates a monopoly for domestic produce is in effect dictating to people how best to employ their capital, and as such is a harmful regulation. If domestic produce can be bought as cheaply as that of foreign industry, such a regulation is obviously useless. If it cannot, the regulation will generally be harmful. No one would build a house that it would cost less for them to buy; just as a tailor does not decide to make his own shoes but buys them from the shoe store.

Likewise, if a foreign country can supply a commodity cheaper than it can be produced at home, it makes more sense to buy a foreign product. A country's industry always grows in proportion to the capital invested in it; this capital will therefore be invested to its maximum advantage.

It goes without saying that is not invested to its maximum advantage if used to purchase an object abroad that can be produced cheaper at home.

The natural advantages a country has over another in terms of producing specific commodities are sometimes so great that the country has a significant edge over its competitors. To produce wine in Scotland, for example, would cost around thirty times the amount it costs to buy it from foreign markets; as such, it would not be beneficial to start producing wine in Scotland. The same can be said with regard to paying higher wages. As long as one country has these advantages and another wants them, it will always be more advantageous to buy than to produce.

Merchants and manufacturers benefit the most from monopoly of the home market. Implementing laws prohibiting the importation of foreign corn and cattle in fact ensures that the country's population and industry never exceed what its own land can maintain.

Luxury goods are the most easily transported. If the importation of foreign goods was not prohibited, several home industries would suffer and even go bankrupt. There are two cases in which such prohibitions are absolutely necessary. The first is the development of a particular industry that is necessary for the defense of the country. The Navigation Act of Britain gave sailors and the shipping industry a monopoly over their own country's trade by:

prohibiting non-British-owned ships and crews from trading with the British settlements, plantations and coastal areas;

excluding or imposing hefty taxes on goods imported in ships of the country in which they were produced; for example, the Dutch were excluded from importing to Britain the goods of any other European country. Though Britain and the Netherlands were not actually at war, there was violent animosity between the two nations.

The second is for a reciprocal tax to safeguard merchants and businesses against being undercut in their home market.

# Chapter III
## Of the Extraordinary Restraints upon the Importing of Goods of Almost all Kinds, from those Countries with which the Balance Is Supposed to be Disadvantageous

### Part I

On the Unreasonableness of those Restraints, even upon the Principles of the Commercial System.

The second method employed by the trading system to keep gold and silver in a country was by placing restraints on the importation of goods from countries with which the balance of trade is disadvantageous. These included lighter tariffs, rarely exceeding 5%, for certain nations, while France's goods were taxed 75%—equivalent to a prohibition. As a result, France imposed heavy taxes on our goods, resulting in a breakdown in trading relations between the two countries, with smugglers now the principal importers of French goods into Britain.

This situation arose out of national prejudice and animosity and is unreasonable in a commercial system. Even though free trade between France and Britain would mean the balance of trade would be in France's favor, it would not be disadvantageous to Britain. If France's wines are better and cheaper than those of Portugal, it would be advantageous for Britain to purchase wine from France rather than Portugal. Though the value of individual goods imported from France would be increased, the overall total value would be decreased, since French goods of the same quality were cheaper than those of another country. This would be the case even if the imported French goods were entirely for home consumption in Britain, but part of them might be re-exported to other countries and sold at a profit, perhaps covering the initial cost of the imported goods. This was the case with the East India trade: though goods were bought with gold, a portion of them were re-exported to other countries for more gold than the initial cost.

### Part II

On the Unreasonableness of those extraordinary Restraints upon other Principles

The notion of imposing restraints and other trade regulations to regulate balance of trade is absurd. The notion that when two countries trade and the balance of trade is even neither loses nor gains, but that if balance is in favor of one or the other country, then one will lose and the other gain is false.

Trade under free market conditions, without the imposition of taxes or the constraints of monopolies, is always advantageous, though not necessarily in equal proportion to each country, in terms of the exchangeable value of the annual produce of the land and labor of the country. If there is an equal balance in the home produce traded, each will gain equally and will replace the capital employed in producing this surplus produce.

In a situation where one country is exporting home-produced commodities and another foreign goods, the balance would still be even, with each country exchanging commodities for commodities. Both countries gain, but not equally since the inhabitants of the country importing the home-produced commodities would make a higher profit from this trade. If Britain, for example, imported from France nothing but French-produced commodities, which it paid for with foreign goods such as tobacco rather than home-produced goods, France would made more profit from this transaction than Britain.

Trade between two countries never consists entirely of the exchange of native commodities on both sides, nor of native commodities on one side and foreign goods on the other. Almost all countries exchange partly native and partly foreign goods, with the country trading the most home-produced and least foreign goods always making the most profit.

If, on the other hand, Britain paid for these French imports with gold rather than tobacco, the balance of trade would be uneven since the commodities are being paid for with gold rather than exchanged for other commodities. Once again, both countries would benefit but France more so than Britain. The profit made by Britain would be employed in producing further goods with which to purchase gold, thus replacing that employed. Britain's capital would be no less as a result of this exportation of gold and silver than it would with the exportation of an equal value of any other commodity; on the contrary, its capital would generally be increased.

Tariffs imposed by Britain on the wine trade appear to favor Portugal over France. The reason for this is it is generally believed that market demand for Britain's produce is greater in Portugal than it is in France. Preferential trade agreements were established between Britain and Portugal. A successful trader will buy his produce where it is cheap and good quality. These monopolies and trade agreements have led to suspicion and prejudice between trading nations, with each considering its neighbor a competitor—when in fact it is in every man's interest to buy whatever he wants from whomever sells it cheapest.

Just as it is in the interests of freemen to hinder the rest of the inhabitants from employing any workmen but themselves, it is in the interest of a country's merchants and manufacturers to secure the monopoly of the home market—leading to heavy duties being placed by Great Britain and most other European countries on almost all imported goods, with high duties and prohibitions on foreign competitors, and restraints upon imported goods from countries with which trade was thought to be disadvantageous.

Trade between France and Britain has been subjected to many prohibitions and restraints. If these two countries were to focus on their own interests, without mercantile jealousy or national animosity, France's commerce might be more advantageous to Britain than that of any other country—and vice versa. France is Britain's nearest neighbor. Even between the parts of France and Britain most remote from each other, returns would be made at least once in the year—at least three times greater than that for trade with the North American colonies, which experience returns only every three to five years. Furthermore, France's population stands at twenty-four million, compared to three million in the North American colonies, and France is a far wealthier country than North America, despite its large numbers of poor and beggars, which is due to the unequal distribution of riches.

Despite the popular notion that an unfavorable balance of trade will result in a country's ruin, this is not the case, as no European country has been negatively affected. On the contrary, balance of trade between two countries is always advantageous.

There is another balance, very different to the balance of trade, which does indeed affect a nation's prosperity or demise: the balance between production and consumption. If the exchangeable value of production exceeds that of consumption, a society's capital will increase proportionately; in this case, the society is living within its revenue. If annual produce falls short of annual consumption, a society's capital will diminish each year.

This balance of production and consumption is entirely different from the balance of trade. It may be constantly in favor of a nation, even if the balance of trade is against it. A nation may have been importing to a greater value than it exports for the past fifty years, yet its real wealth, the exchangeable value of the annual produce of its lands and labor, may have been increasing in a much greater proportion.

# Chapter IV
## Of Drawbacks

### Summary:

Merchants and manufacturers are keen to sell their goods to the most extensive foreign market possible. Since their home country has no jurisdiction in foreign markets, they do not have any monopoly there. As a result, they petition their governments to create incentives for export. Drawbacks are one such incentive and perhaps the most reasonable (rebate of taxes or duties paid on imported goods that have been re-exported).

Enabling a merchant to recuperate the excise or inland duty imposed upon his domestic industry does not direct a greater quantity of goods to be exported than would have been had no duty been imposed. Such incentives tend to preserve the natural division and distribution of labor in a society.

Before the revolt of our North American colonies, we had the monopoly of the tobacco production in Maryland and Virginia. In order to facilitate export of surplus tobacco, drawbacks were introduced, provided the export took place within three years.

We still have the monopoly over sugar production in the West Indian islands. If sugar is exported within a year, therefore, all import duties importing are drawn back.

Some goods are prohibited from importation; they may be imported and stored for export, upon payment of duties, but there will be no drawbacks for exportation once they are exported.

# Chapter V
## Of Bounties

## Summary:

(Digression concerning the Corn Trade and Corn Laws ignored)

Bounties upon exportation are frequently used in Britain, enabling the merchants of certain domestic products to sell their goods as cheaply as their competitors in the foreign market.

Since foreigners cannot be forced to buy a country's goods, they are encouraged to do so by the use of bounties. In this way, the mercantile system aimed to enrich the whole country by establishing balance of trade.

Bounties should be granted only to those trades which cannot be executed without them. But in every branch of trade in which the price the goods fetch covers the ordinary profits of stock as well as the capital employed by the merchant in preparing and sending the goods to market, bounties are not required.

The only trades that actually require bounties are those in which a merchant is obliged to sell his goods for less than it cost him to bring them to market. The bounty is given in order to make up this loss, thus encouraging him to continue or perhaps trade in goods of which the expense is greater than the returns. If this practice were to continue over a period of time, there would be no capital left in the country.

Trading using bounties is the only situation in which one country is always the loser as it sells its goods for less than it cost to bring them to market. If the bounty does not repay to the merchant what he would otherwise have lost on the price of his goods, he would soon find a trade in which the price of his goods would cover this. Bounties are harmful since, over time, they force a country to trade in a way which greatly disadvantages it.

The average price of corn (wheat) has fallen considerably since the establishment of the bounty. But this happened in spite of the bounty, not as a consequence of it—as demonstrated in the case of France, where corn prices fell despite the fact that France had no bounties, although exportation of corn was subjected to a general prohibition until 1764. This gradual fall in the average price of grain is probably due to the gradual rise in the real value of silver; it would appear that bounties never contribute to lowering the price of grain.

In years of abundance, the bounty, by encouraging exportation, maintains corn prices in the home market above what they would normally fall to. Indeed, this was the objective. During years of scarcity, although the bounty is frequently suspended, the volume of exports during years of plenty in fact hinders the abundance of one year from relieving the scarcity of another. Consequently, bounties raise the price of corn in the home market during times of abundance as well as times scarcity.

Expansion of foreign markets through bounties always comes at a loss to the home market since commodities exported thanks to a bounty would otherwise not have been exported but would have remained in the home market, thus increasing home consumption and lowering the price of that commodity. Bounties impose two taxes on those using them: a tax on payment of the bounty and a tax on the resulting higher price of the commodity in the home market. In the case of corn, for example, since it is a commodity bought by the entire population, this tax is paid by each citizen.

In reality, the effect of a bounty is not so much that it raises the nominal value of corn, but rather that it decreases the value of silver, since the amount of silver that corn (or any other commodity, particularly home-produced) exchanges for is increased.

The price of corn regulates that of all other such commodities. Consequently, corn also regulates the monetary price of labor, which must always be sufficient to enable a worker to purchase enough corn to maintain him and his family, be it in a liberal, moderate, or meager manner, depending on the current state of the society in which he lives.

With regard to encouraging the production of a specific commodity, a bounty on production is more effective than one on exportation since it lowers the price of the commodity in the home market. As such, the bounty, rather than imposing a second tax upon the population, reimburses them indirectly for what they contributed to the first tax. Bounties upon production were very rarely granted. The prejudices inherent to the commercial system led to a belief that national wealth is more directly related to exportation than production. As such, exportation has been favored as the more immediate means of bringing money into the country. It is a well-known fact that bounties on exportation have been abused over time, yet they are the most popular aspect of the mercantile system. I have known parties to agree privately amongst themselves to grant a bounty out of their own pockets upon the exportation of their goods.

This method proved so successful that it more than doubled the price of their goods in the home market, notwithstanding a very considerable increase in the produce.

Something similar to a bounty upon production was nevertheless granted occasionally. The tonnage bounties for the white herring and whale fisheries are one such case. They tend to render the goods cheaper in the home market than they would otherwise be. In all other respects, their effects are the same as those of bounties upon exportation. These tonnage bounties result in a part of the country's capital being employed in bringing goods to market, the price of which does not repay the cost, together with the ordinary profits of stock.

Although these tonnage bounties for fisheries do not contribute to a nation's wealth, they contribute indirectly towards its defense, since they increase the number of sailors and shipping industries. As such, these bounties could be viewed as a cheaper means of contributing towards the nation's defense than establishing and maintaining an official navy.

Despite these positive aspects, however, the legislature governing the granting of these bounties had some negative aspects too. Firstly, the herring shipping bounty was too great, and the herrings were sometimes cured using Scotch or foreign salt, both of which were delivered, free of excise duty, to the fish-curers. Secondly, the bounty for the white-herring fishery is a tonnage bounty, calculated in proportion to the ship's cargo rather than the company's diligence or success in the fishery industry, with the result that these companies were often more focused on obtaining the bounty than on operating conscientiously. Thirdly, the fishing method for which this tonnage bounty in the white herring industry was granted (by ships containing twenty to eighty tons of cargo) was not as well adapted to, for example, Scotland as it was to the Netherlands, the country in which this method originated. Fourthly, in many parts of Scotland, at certain times of the year herrings are a staple of the daily diet of many lower-income families. A bounty which lowered the price of herrings in the home market would significantly help these struggling families. But unfortunately the herring shipping bounty made no such contribution. Rather, it has ruined the fishery industry, which is by far the best adapted for the supply of the home market, with the additional bounty of 2s:8d per barrel for exportation resulting in the majority (over two-thirds) of the produce of the fishery industry going abroad.

A bounty is sometimes no more than a drawback, and consequently is not liable to the same objections as is a true bounty. The bounty, for example, upon refined exported sugar is a drawback of the duties upon the brown and Muscovado sugars from which it is made. Once the sugar has been refined and altered through manufacture, this drawback is called a bounty.

# Chapter VI
## Of Treaties of Commerce

### Summary:

When a nation enters into preferential trade agreements with other countries, either permitting the entry of certain goods from just one foreign country, or exempting the goods of just one country from duties, the merchants and manufacturers involved are at a significant advantage over others, enjoying a form of monopoly in the country favoring them.

Although these preferential trade agreements favor these merchants and manufacturers, they disfavor the countries receiving the goods of these individuals. By granting a monopoly to a foreign nation, a country's citizens are forced to pay more for foreign goods than they would in the case of free competition. The purchasing power of the nation's annual produce in terms of buying foreign goods consequently diminishes, since there is an imbalance between the nominal and natural prices of the foreign goods. A country therefore loses purchasing power as a result of these preferential trade agreements.

A country sometimes grants a monopoly to a foreign nation for specific goods in the belief that, in the overall commerce between the countries involved, it will in fact sell more than it would buy, therefore procuring a greater amount of gold and silver than it would have otherwise. It was on this basis that the trade agreement between Britain and Portugal was established, with Portugal agreeing to admit Britain's woolen goods, and Britain Portugal's wine, with no customs duty.

Annually, Portugal receives a greater quantity of gold from Brazil than can be employed in its domestic commerce. The surplus must be exchanged for something for which there is a more advantageous market at home. A large share of it comes annually to Britain, in return for English commodities.

The annual importation of gold and silver is employed in foreign trade, which can be carried out more advantageously by means of these metals than of other goods since it costs less to transport them from one place to another, and they do not lose value during transportation, unlike certain commodities. Of all the commodities bought in one foreign country with the sole intent of being sold or exchanged for goods in another country, gold and silver is the most convenient.

When a commodity is taxed, although the merchant involved advances the money, he does not truly pay the tax as he recovers it in the price of the commodity. At the end of the day, the tax is paid by the end consumer. But money is a commodity, of which every man is a merchant; nobody buys it with a view solely to selling it again, and it has no end consumer.

# Chapter VII
## Of Colonies

### Part I

Of the Motives for Establishing New Colonies.

The motives for the establishment of the first European colonies in America and the West Indies were not as plain and distinct as for those in ancient Greece and Rome.

States in ancient Greece possessed only small territories, which led to overpopulation, with the result that inhabitants were sent elsewhere.

In response to the large demand for land ownership amongst Roman citizens, Rome assigned people land in the conquered provinces of Italy, where they remained subject to Rome's legislation. The colony established a garrison in a newly conquered province.

A Roman colony was altogether different from a Greek one. Even the word "colony" has a very different meaning in the two languages: the Latin word (colonia) signifies simply "a plantation;" the Greek word (apoikia) signifies "a home far away from home." Both institutions derived their origin either from necessity or utility.

The European colonies in America and the West Indies were not established out of necessity, although they have since proven highly useful. When they were first established, this was not expected and was not the motive behind their establishment.

The discovery of the West Indies was made by a Genoese sailor, who undertook the daring project of sailing to the East Indies by the west. In letters to Isabella de Castile and Ferdinand of Aragon, he called the countries which he had discovered "The Indies." The staple diet of the inhabitants of these islands – Indian corn, yams, potatoes and bananas— were vegetables as yet unknown in Europe.

Further voyages of discovery of "the New World" by the Spanish, subsequent to those of Columbus, seem to have been motivated by the thirst for gold. Upon arrival at any unknown coast, the adventurers' first inquiry was always whether there was any gold to be found there—and depending on the reply, they either left or settled in the newly discovered country. Indeed, the main motivation behind these voyages of discovery was the prospect of gold and silver mines.

The first English settlers in North America offered the king a fifth of all the gold and silver found there, as a motive for granting them their patents. Sir Waiter Raleigh, companies in London and Plymouth, as well as the council of Plymouth also paid this sum. However, these first settlers' expectations of finding gold and silver mines, as well as of discovering a north-west passage to the East Indies, did not come to fruition.

## Part II

Causes of the Prosperity of New Colonies

A colony established by a developed country on land that has few or no inhabitants will grow wealthy more quickly than that of any other type of society.

The colonists bring with them a sound knowledge of agriculture and other useful arts, and a basic knowledge of their country's governance (the judicial laws and systems in place), which they deploy and establish in the new settlement.

Each colonist gains a greater surface of land than he could possibly ever cultivate and is not weighed down by rent or taxes. With almost the entirety of his produce being for his own benefit, the colonist is motivated to work hard to produce as much and as efficiently as possible.

In fact, the amount of land is generally so vast that he will seldom be able to use it to its maximum potential, often not reaping even a tenth of what it could yield. In order to capitalize as much as possible from his land, a landowner will hire as many workers as possible and generally pay good wages. But these workers tend to leave and become landlords themselves, in turn employing other workers, who soon leave them for the same reason.

High wages tend to go hand in hand with an increased number of marriages, with children often following in their father's footsteps. In new colonies, productive, fertile land can be bought very cheaply. Consequently, high wages lead to population growth, and the low prices for land encourage cultivation and improvement, enabling the landowner to pay high wages—all of which lead to real wealth and power.

From the time of the earliest settlements, the Spanish colonies were strictly controlled by their mother country, while those of the other European nations were for a long time left to their own devices. Before the Spanish Conquest, there was no cattle fit for draught—the lama was the only animal used for this purpose—and they had no knowledge of ploughs or even the use of iron.

The Swedes established themselves in New Jersey, but, left to their own devices by Sweden, the colony was soon swallowed up by the Dutch colony of New York, which in 1674 fell under the authority of the English. The Dutch settlements were originally governed by a single company. The colony of Nova Belgia, which is divided into two provinces (New York and New Jersey), would probably have prospered even if it had remained under the governance of the Dutch; at present, the company has the monopoly of the direct trade from Africa to America, which consists almost entirely of the slave trade.

The French colony of Canada was controlled by a single company until the English gained possession of this country. But no colonies have progressed more rapidly than the English colonies in North America. Plenty of good land and the freedom to manage their own affairs seem to be two major factors in new colonies' prosperity. This is demonstrated in the case of Spain and Portugal, which possess a better quality of land than the English colonies of North America, yet the latter prospered more because the English political institutions were more favorable to the improvement and cultivation of land.

Colony law stipulates that each landowner has a limited amount of time during which to cultivate and improve his lands—failing which the land will be granted to another person. In Pennsylvania, there is no right of primogeniture, and land is divided equally among children. In three provinces of New Britain, the oldest child receives only a double share; in the other English colonies, the right of primogeniture follows English law.

For a new colony, the abundance and cheapness of productive land are the main factors behind rapid prosperity. The labor of the English colonies is employed in improvement and cultivation of land, resulting in greater and more valuable produce than that of the other three nations, where labor is diverted to other employment. Due to the moderate taxes, a greater proportion of this produce belongs to the colonies themselves, and can be stored up and used to employ further laborers.

Colonists have never contributed to the defense of the mother country or the support of its civil government. They have been defended at the expense of the mother country. Payments made to their civil government have always been very moderate—generally a minimal amount towards paying the salaries of the governor, judges and police officers, and maintaining a few of the most useful public works.

The most important part of government expenditure – that of defense and protection—has constantly fallen upon the mother country. Civil government ceremonies do not involve any expensive pomp, and ecclesiastical government is equally frugal, with no taxes contributing towards the support of Church and clergy unheard of; clergy are maintained either by means of moderate stipends or voluntary contributions.

With regard to the disposal of surplus produce; i.e. what is over and above their own consumption, the English colonies have been more favored than other European nations since they have been granted the most extensive market for exportation. Every European nation has endeavored to monopolize the commerce of its colonies, by implementing measures such as prohibiting ships from foreign nations from trading with them, and prohibiting the colonies themselves from importing foreign European goods. The manner in which this monopoly has been executed has varied greatly from nation to nation.

Some nations handed over the control of their colonies to a single company, from whom the colonists were obliged to purchase the European goods they needed, and to whom they were obliged to sell all of surplus produce.

Other nations limited the commerce of their colonies to a specific port in the mother country, placing restrictions on ships, which were required to purchase an often costly trading license.

Other nations leave their colonies to their own devices, not imposing any restrictions on ports or requirements for trading licenses. In this case, the sheer volume and geographical spread of the traders increases competition and therefore lowers profits. In this free-trade policy, colonies are able both to sell their own produce and buy European goods at a reasonable price. In Britain, this has been the policy since the dissolution of the Plymouth company, in the very early stages of colonization. France, too, has been adhering to this policy since the dissolution of the Mississippi company in Britain. The result is that profits made from trade between France and Britain with the colonies, though higher than they would be in a free competition situation, are far from spectacular—hence prices for European goods are not particularly high in the majority of French and English colonies.

With regard to Britain's colonies exporting their surplus produce, certain commodities had restrictions on them confining them to the market of the mother country. Some of these commodities were known as "enumerated commodities," due to the enumeration process used during transportation. The remainder, the "non-enumerated" goods, could be exported directly to other countries, provided they were transported in British or plantation ships of which the owners and three-quarters of the crew were British subjects.

These non-enumerated commodities included some of the most important productions of America and the West Indies: grain, lumber, salt, fish, sugar and rum. Grain is the major culture within all new colonies. By providing an extensive market for it, the law encourages colonies to extend this cultivation beyond just their own consumption needs, with the result that there is always sufficient to provide for a continually growing population.

In a densely forested country, in which timber is plentiful and therefore of little value, the expense of clearing a forest is a major obstacle to improvement. By providing an extensive market for colonies' timber, the law endeavors to facilitate improvement by raising the price of a commodity which would otherwise be of little value, enabling them to make a profit from something that would otherwise have cost them money.

Countries with a low population density tend to have a surplus of cattle above and beyond their consumption needs, and as such the cattle are of little value. In order for a country to be improved, the price of cattle must be on a par with that of corn; by providing an extensive market for American cattle, the law endeavors to raise its value.

Legislature focused heavily on increasing Britain's shipping and naval power by extending its colonies' fisheries. The New Britain fishery was one of the world's most sizeable fisheries. To this day, the whale fishery in New Britain operates for the most part without any bounties. Fish is a major export commodity from North America to Spain, Portugal, and the Mediterranean.

Sugar was originally an enumerated commodity, which could only be exported to Britain. But after the lobby by sugar-planters in 1751, its exportation was permitted worldwide; however, the restrictions imposed on its exportation, coupled with the high price of sugar in Britain, rendered this measure ineffectual. Britain and its colonies remain to this day practically the sole market for all sugar produced in the British plantations.

Rum is a major export commodity from America to the coast of Africa, where it is traded for Negro slaves.

If America's entire surplus produce, including grain, salt and fish, had been enumerated and thereby forced into Britain's market, it would have interfered significantly with the latter's home industry. Prompted most likely by resentment about this interference, rather than a concern for America's interests, major commodities were not only kept out of the enumeration process, but the importation into Britain of all grain (with the exception of rice) and all salt provisions was prohibited.

There are two sorts of enumerated commodities. Firstly, those native to America, which cannot be or are not produced in the mother country. These include molasses, coffee, cocoa-nuts, tobacco, pimento, ginger, whale fins, raw silk, cotton, wool, beaver, and other animal pelts of America, indigo, fustic, and other dyeing woods. Secondly, those not native to America, but which are and can be produced in the mother country, though not in sufficient quantities to meet demand, which is principally supplied from foreign countries. These include naval stores, masts, yards and bowsprits, tar, pitch, and turpentine, pig and bar iron, copper ore, hides and skins, pot and pearl ashes.

Even a heavy importation of commodities of the first group would not discourage the growth or interfere with the sale of any of the mother country's produce. By confining these goods to the home market, it was believed that merchants would be able to buy them for less in the plantations and consequently sell them for a better profit at home; and also that this would establish good trading relations between the plantations and foreign countries, of which Britain was to be the centre or emporium, as the European country into which these commodities were first imported.

The free trade arrangement between the British colonies of America and the West Indies, both in enumerated and non-enumerated commodities, works perfectly, with each finding an extensive market for all of its produce.

Britain's liberal views towards trade by its colonies apply mainly to goods in their crude state or in the first stage of manufacture. More advanced and refined goods were reserved for Britain, and laws were established to prevent their manufacture within the colonies, through measures such as high duties and sometimes prohibition.

Although Britain encourages the manufacture of pig and bar iron in America by exempting these products of import duties, it prohibits the establishment of any steel furnaces or slit-mills in its American plantations, requiring the colonies to purchase these goods from the home country's merchants and forbidding them to work themselves in these more refined industries.

Britain also prohibits the exportation of American produce from one province to another, be it by water, horseback or cart, of hats, wools and woolen goods – a regulation which effectively prevents the manufacture of such commodities for distant sale, confining the colonies' industry to basic household commodities.

Although these prohibitions may be unjust, they did not negatively affect the colonies. Land there is still so cheap, and consequently labor so costly, that they can import from the mother country almost all of the more refined goods for less than they could produce them themselves.

In everything except foreign trade, the English colonists were free to manage their own affairs, which were conducted in the same manner as business in the mother country, overseen by an assembly of representatives of the people, who are the body responsible for imposing taxes paid to the colony government.

In all European colonies, sugar-cane cultivation is carried out by Negro slaves. The profit and success of the plantations is directly dependent on the good management of these slaves—and in this respect, the French are significantly superior to the English.

The law, which provides only weak protection to the slave against violence from his master, is likely to be better adhered to in a colony in which government is arbitrary than in one where it is free. In countries with established laws on slavery, magistrates often intervene in a master's management of his slaves—whereas in a free country, where the master is perhaps a member of the colony assembly or an elector of such a member, magistrates do not tend to intervene, with this hierarchy making it more difficult for them to protect the slave.

A compassionate approach to managing slaves renders them not only more faithful but more intelligent – and ultimately more useful. Such slaves act more as free servants, often with integrity and concern for their masters' interests—virtues generally more associated with free servants, and which will never be seen in a slave who is treated as slaves commonly are in countries in which the master is free and secure.

## Part III

Of the Advantages which Europe has derived From the Discovery of America

America's discovery and colonization provided other countries with an extensive market for their surplus produce.

When trade is limited exclusively to the mother countries, the level of enjoyments and progress of industry is diminished because it decreases consumption, ultimately cramping the industry of the colonies. Consequently, commodities are more expensive for trading partners, which not only excludes other countries from a particular market, but confines colonies to particular markets. There is a great difference between being excluded from a particular market when other markets are open, and being confined to a particular market when others are shut. Colonization has therefore served to increase the enjoyments and progress the industries of Europe, though when trade is limited to the mother countries, the level of enjoyments and progress of industry is decreased below its natural level.

One of the advantages each colonizing country derives from its colonies is the military force they furnish for its defense and the revenue they contribute towards the support of its civil government. America's European colonies have never yet furnished military support to their mother country, with the result that America's military power has never been sufficient to guarantee its colonies' defense. During times of war, the deployment of military forces to defend colonies has historically put a strain on mother countries' military forces. In this respect, therefore, European colonies have been a cause of weakness rather than of strength to their respective mother countries, with the taxes levied on colonies, of Britain in particular, rarely covering the expense incurred even during times of peace, let alone during wartime. Such colonies, therefore, have been a source of expense rather than revenue for their respective mother countries.

The advantages mother countries derive from their colonies are mainly due to agreements on exclusive trade. The surplus produce of the British colonies that is classed as enumerated commodities can be sent only to Britain. Other countries then purchase from Britain. These commodities must be sold for less, therefore, in Britain than in other countries, and must contribute more to increase the enjoyments of Britain than to those of other countries. They must also contribute more towards the progress of Britain's industry. Britain must get a better price for these enumerated commodities than other countries could get for the same commodities produced in their countries. Industries in Britain, for example, will be able to purchase a greater quantity of sugar and tobacco from its colonies than the same industries in foreign countries can purchase. Since both Britain's and other countries' produce is exchanged for sugar and tobacco produced by British colonies, this higher price guarantee ensures that Britain benefits more from this situation.

Britain's monopoly on tobacco from Maryland and Virginia means it obtains it at a lower price than, for example, France, to whom Britain sells a considerable part of it. Had France and other European countries had a free trade agreement with Maryland and Virginia, the prices would likely have dropped, both for these European countries and for Britain.

Britain's monopoly over trade with its colonies, established through the Navigation Acts, meant that foreign capital previously employed in this trade was withdrawn. England's capital that had previously been employed for just part of it was now to cover the entirety. But this was insufficient, and consequently commodities were sold at very high prices. The capital which had previously bought just part of the colonies' surplus produce was now employed to buy the entirety—but it could not buy such a volume at anything near the old price, and therefore bought at cheaper prices. The merchants benefited from this, buying cheap and selling for a high price, making a higher profit than the usual rate.

Britain's monopoly over its colonies' external trade, and the fact that the country's capital has not increased in proportion to this trade, has meant that it has had to withdraw from other branches of trade part of the capital previously employed in them, in order to employ it in its colony trade. Consequently, colony trade has increased, while many other branches of foreign trade have diminished. The country's commodities intended for foreign sale, instead of being traded with neighboring European markets, as was the case prior to the Navigation Acts, have been traded instead with the colonies—the market in which they have the monopoly, rather than to that in which they have many competitors. As such, the demise of foreign trade is a direct result of the extensive growth of colony trade; these other branches of trade have naturally suffered as a result of the country drawing some of its mercantile capital from them and investing it in its colonies.

# Chapter VIII
## Conclusion of the Mercantile System

## Summary:

The mercantile system, by encouraging exportation and discouraging importation, gives a country's laborers an advantage, enabling them to undersell those in foreign markets.

Measures used to encourage the importation of materials for manufacture include exemption from duties to which other goods are subject, and bounties for goods from the British colonies, mainly restricted to American plantations.

The first such bounties were granted on the importation of naval stores from America, which included timber for masts, yards, and bowsprits; hemp, tar, pitch, and turpentine. The second bounty was on indigo from the British plantations. Others, which were granted at the time Britain started to experience problems with its American colonies, were on the importation of hemp, undressed flax and wood from America; raw silk, pipe, hogshead, and barrel-staves from the British plantations; and hemp from Ireland. Britain viewed the wealth of its American colonies as belonging to the mother country.

Some of the measures used to discourage the exportation of materials for manufacture include full prohibitions and high duties. The inland wool trade, for example, is subject to onerous and heavy restrictions; for instance, wool can only be packaged in packs of leather or pack-cloth, labeled "WOOL" or "YARN;" it cannot be loaded on any horse or cart, or physically transported by land within five miles of the coast at night. These regulations are in force throughout Britain.

The effect of these regulations has been to lower the price of British wool – which, indeed, was the purpose of the regulations. To negatively affect the interests of one group of citizens just to promote another, however, is unjust.

The exportation of all goods for manufacture was rendered duty free, except for instruments of trade. In the case of coal, which is used both in manufacture and as an instrument of trade, heavy export duties were imposed—which in fact amounted to more than the original value of the commodity at the coalmine.

The exportation of instruments of trade was restrained by prohibitions; the exportation of frames and engines for knitting woolen goods was prohibited, as were tools used in the manufacture of cotton, linen, woolen and silk.

A person who poaches a skilled craftsman from a British manufacturer to go and work abroad, whether to exercise or teach his trade, is liable to be fined up to a thousand pounds and subject to two years' imprisonment. Any craftsman who moves abroad to exercise or teach his trade must return within six months—otherwise he will forfeit his land, goods, and chattels to the king and will be declared an alien in every respect, no longer eligible for the king's protection.

Man's liberty is so plainly sacrificed by the futile interests of our merchants and manufacturers. The motive of all these regulations is to extend our country's industries—not by improving them but by repressing our neighbors and destroying competition.

But the laws governing our American and West Indian colonies sacrifice the interests of the home consumer in favor of those of the producer. Indeed, a whole empire has been established for the sole purpose of obliging consumers to buy from the homeland's producers, to benefit these producers. But the slight profit this monopoly ensures our producers is paid for heavily by the home consumers, who contribute towards the maintenance and defense of the empire.

As a result, the last two last wars incurred expenses of over two hundred million with a new debt of over a hundred and seventy million over and above that spent during previous wars. The interest of this debt alone amounts to more than the profit made through the monopoly of the colony trade—indeed, it surpasses the entire value of the colony trade, or the whole value of the goods annually exported to the colonies.

# Chapter IX
## Of The Agricultural Systems, Or Of Those Systems Of Political Economy Which Represent The Produce Of Land, As Either The Sole Or The Principal Source Of The Revenue And Wealth Of Every Country

### Summary:

The line of thought, particularly amongst scholars in France, was that agricultural development was the sole source of a country's revenue and wealth. Mr. Colbert, the famous minister of Louis XIV, however, embraced all of the prejudices of the mercantile system, and regulated the country's industry and commerce on the same model as that of departments of a public office, rather than allowing men free rein. He prohibited the exportation of corn and excluded the country's inhabitants from foreign trade, thus discouraging and suppressing the country's agriculture, favoring industry over agriculture.

His thinking was directly opposed to that of the French scholars who believed that agricultural development represented the basis of a country's wealth; whereas Mr. Colbert's line of thought favored industry over agriculture, these French intellectuals favored agriculture over industry.

Under Mr. Colbert's system, people were divided into three classes: landowners, cultivators (the productive class), artificers and merchants (the unproductive class).

Landowners contribute to production by investing in improving the land, buildings, drains, enclosures, etc. (ground expenses).

Cultivators contribute by investing in instruments of husbandry, cattle, seed, and maintenance of the farmer's family, servants and cattle. The produce of the land left over for the farmer once he has paid the rent should to be sufficient to cover all of his expenses, together with ordinary profits. Under this system, initial outlay expenses and annual expenses are called "productive expenses" since they go towards the end net produce. The ground expenses of the landlord, together with the original outlay and annual expenses of the farmer, are the only three expenses deemed productive.

Under this system, all other expenses and all other classes of people, even those who are the most productive, are viewed as unproductive. Artificers and manufacturers in particular, whose work significantly improves the crude produce of the land, are viewed as barren and unproductive under this system.

The capital error of this system is its inaccurate representation of the class consisting of craftsmen, manufacturers and merchants as altogether barren and unproductive.

This system, with all its imperfections, has numerous followers, particularly the economists of France. Literature on this system was nevertheless the nearest approximation to the truth published at that time on the subject of political economy, and as such provides valuable information for anyone studying the principles of this topic. Although its suggestion that agricultural labor is the only productive labor is a somewhat narrow and confined notion, its recognition that a nation's wealth consists not of the money but rather of the consumable goods produced annually by the labor of its society is a better, more liberal notion.

The Netherlands draws a great part of its subsistence from other countries; live cattle from Holstein and Jutland, and corn from all over Europe. A trading and manufacturing country is able to purchase a large volume of unfinished produce from other countries with just a small part of its own manufactured produce. On the contrary, a country with no trade or manufacturing is generally obliged to use a major part of its own produce to purchase a very small part of other countries' manufactured produce.

European countries' political economy favors manufacturing industries and foreign trade over agriculture, whereas other countries have tended to favor agriculture over manufacturing industries and foreign trade.

The major form of commerce of every nation is that between the inhabitants of the town and the country. The town purchases unfinished produce from the country, which it pays for by returning a portion of it manufactured and prepared for immediate use. The trade between these two different sets of people involves unfinished crude produce being exchanged for manufactured produce. When prices of manufactured goods rise, those of crude land-produced goods drop, thereby discouraging agriculture. When the number of craftsmen and manufacturers drops, the home market tends to diminish. Since this is the most important market for home-produced crude produce, agriculture is further discouraged.

The systems which favor agriculture and impose restraints on manufacturing and foreign trade indirectly discourage the very industry they are aiming to promote. They are more inconsistent than the mercantile system, which, by encouraging manufacturing and foreign trade over agriculture, channels a portion of a society's capital away from a more profitable industry towards a less profitable one.

Any system which endeavors to channel a greater share of capital towards a particular industry than would naturally go to it is actually going against the very process it is endeavoring to promote. This approach hinders rather than accelerates a society's progress towards real wealth and power, diminishing the real value of the annual produce of its land and labor.

When a system of either preferential agreements or restrictions is removed, a system of natural liberty establishes itself of its own accord. Any man, as long as he does not break the law, is left free to pursue his own interests in his own way, and to compete with others through industry and capital.

## Appendix To Book IV

Tonnage Bounty to the White herring Fishery.

An account of busses equipped in Scotland for eleven years, with the number of empty barrels carried out and the number of barrels of herrings caught; also the average bounty for each barrel of sea-sticks and on each full barrel.

# Book V

The Revenue of the Sovereign or Commonwealth

## Chapter I
### Of The Expenses of the Sovereign or Commonwealth

### Part I

Of the Expense of Defense.

The most important duty of a sovereign is to protect his society from violence and invasion. This is ensured by means of military force.

Agricultural workers, used to the rugged life of outdoor labor, are well equipped to prepare themselves for war. Furthermore, if war occurs after the sowing season and before harvest time, farm workers can be spared without too much loss to the business. In a more advanced society, the progress of industry and the evolution of war over time mean that it would be impossible for citizens to go to war at their own expense. In a country in which the majority of the citizens are craftsmen and manufacturers, the majority of the people who go to war must be drawn from these citizens, and therefore maintained by the public.

In a lengthy war, it becomes necessary for the public to maintain those in the army. The number of citizens who can go to war must therefore never exceed what a society can maintain. As a rule of thumb for modern European nations, no more than one-hundredth of the total population of a country can be employed as soldiers.

With the evolution of warfare, the question is raised as to whether the army should be a professional standing army employing a specific class of citizens. Division of labor is implemented in an army to improve its efficiency, as with every other form of employment.

A state may opt to enforce a professional, standing, army or may train its citizens for a limited time and maintain a militia. The practice of military exercises is the sole or principal occupation of the soldiers in a standing army, and they receive maintenance or pay from the state for their subsistence.

A militia that has served during successive wars becomes in every respect a standing army. The soldiers are exercised daily in the use of firearms, and, being constantly under the command of their officers, are used to the same form of strict regime as that in the standing armies.

The most important duty of a sovereign, therefore, grows gradually more expensive as the society develops. The military force of the society, which originally cost the sovereign no expense, must be maintained by him during war as well as times of peace.

The introduction of firearms has brought with it much expense, with both arms and ammunition prices on the rise. A musket is more costly than a javelin; a cannon and mortar are not only more expensive but much heavier machines, making them more costly both in terms of purchase price and transportation costs.

## Part II.

Of the Expense of Justice

The second duty of the sovereign is to protect each member of society from injustice or oppression. This involves two very different degrees of expense.

Inequality between the rich and poor, with the wealthy owning grand properties, incites resentment amongst the poor. In this situation, implementing a civil magistrate provides peace of mind for the owner of the valuable property. The acquisition of property therefore requires the establishment of a civil government, which grants power to educated professionals, particularly older individuals, who command more respect than the young, as well as wealthy individuals and those from established families.

The judicial authority of the sovereign, far from being a cause of expense, was for a long time a source of revenue. Citizens seeking justice were willing to pay for it, with gifts from the requesting party being commonplace. Individuals found guilty were required to compensate both the prosecuting party as well as a fine to the sovereign.

With the introduction of compulsory taxes for judicial services, the giving of gifts was prohibited. Judges were paid fixed salaries, and since the taxes more than compensated the sovereign, the justice system was administered gratis.

The expense for justice could have been covered by the court fees, without exposing the administration of justice to potential corruption, but it is difficult to regulate court fees when a person of such high power as the sovereign contributes to them. Court fees were originally the main source of maintenance for Britain's courts of justice, with each court endeavoring to attract as much business as possible.

Impartial administration of justice is necessary in a society, to protect each individual's liberty and to provide security. In order to ensure individuals' rights are respected, the judicial system needs to be separate and independent from executive power. Executive power should not have any authority to remove a judge from office, nor should it control the payment of his salary.

## Part III.

Of the Expense of Public Works and Public Institutions.

The third duty of the sovereign is to establish and maintain the public institutions and public works the profit of which does not cover their expenses. Institutions of this kind are chiefly involved in facilitating commerce and promoting education.

The expense involved in building and maintaining public works that facilitate a country's commerce, such as roads, bridges, canals, harbors, etc., varies. The cost of constructing and maintaining public roads increases in line with the volume and weight of goods transported on them. The strength of a bridge must be suited to the number and weight of vehicles likely to pass over it. The depth and the supply of water for a navigable canal must be appropriate for the number and tonnage of the vessels likely to transport goods on it, and the extent of a harbor will depend on the volume of ships that will dock there.

The majority of public works can be managed so as to bring in revenue sufficient to cover their expenses without burdening society. Transport facilities can be constructed and maintained by charging a small toll on the vehicles using them; coinage provides a small revenue to the sovereign; the post office provides a considerable revenue.

In some parts of Europe, the toll or lock duty on a canal is given to private individuals, who then have a personal interest in the upkeep of the canal since if it is not properly maintained, navigation will cease— and with it their profit. If tolls are managed by commissioners who have no personal interest in them, they may well be less attentive to the maintenance of the works. An example is the tolls for the upkeep of a highway, which cannot be made the property of private individuals; the proprietors of these tolls often neglect the repair and maintenance of the road, yet continue to levy the same tolls. It is therefore preferable for such tolls to be managed by commissioners or trustees. Government, by taking the management of the turnpikes into its own hands, could employ soldiers to keep the roads in good order. If government neglected the reparation of the highways, it would be difficult to impose the turnpike tolls, with the result that the high levies charged to the people would not actually be used for their intended purpose.

Public works that are confined to a particular place or district are better managed by a local administration than by the state. If the streets of London were lit and paved at the expense of the treasury, would they be so well lit and paved as they are at present?

Of the public Works and Institution which are necessary for facilitating particular Branches of Commerce.

The object of public works and institutions is to facilitate commerce in general. But in order to facilitate a particular branch of trade, specific institutions are necessary. When commerce is conducted with barbarous nations, protection is required for those involved. English and French East Indian companies were authorized to erect forts for this purpose. Certain countries, however, did not authorize the building of such fortified places within their territory, and what tended to happen in this situation was that an "ambassador" was elected who mediated disputes between the companies and the natives—his character affording the traders protection. The Turkey Company employed such an ambassador in Constantinople. The first British embassies to Russia were established out of commercial interests.

It seems logical that the considerable expense of this protection for a particular branch of commerce should be paid for through a duty imposed on the commodities involved. This protection of trade, for the most part from pirates and freebooters, is said to have been the origin of what we now know as customs duties.

The protection of trade is viewed as essential to the defense of the Commonwealth, and is the responsibility of the authorities. The collection and application of customs duties has therefore always fallen to the authorities, but some nations have deviated from this, with merchants in parts of Europe persuading the legislature to entrust this responsibility to them, resulting in them subsequently mismanaging or confining the trade.

Regulated companies resemble in every respect the trade corporations that are so common throughout Europe—a sort of enlarged monopoly of the same form. The regulated foreign-trade companies currently operating in Britain are the ancient merchant-adventurers company, now known as the Hamburg Company, the Russia Company, the Eastland Company, the Turkey Company, and the African Company.

Terms of admission into the Hamburg Company are said to be fairly straightforward, and the directors do not have the power to impose restraints or regulations on the trade conducted.

The Turkey Company previously charged an admission fee of twenty-five pounds for persons below the age of twenty-six, and fifty pounds for persons above that age. Only merchants were permitted admission, with a restriction excluding all shopkeepers and retailers. A bylaw stipulated that British commodities could only be exported to Turkey in the company's ships, and since those ships always sailed from the port of London, this restriction confined the trade to that expensive port, and to traders who lived in and around London. Another bylaw stipulated that no person living within twenty miles of London could become a member. These abuses led to the implementation of the Act of George II, which reduced admission fees, removed age restrictions, and granted merchants and freemen of London the right to export all forms of British goods, from any of Britain's ports to any port in Turkey, against payment of general customs duties in accordance with the laws of the British ambassador and consuls resident in Turkey, and the company's bylaws.

Regulated companies never maintained forts or garrisons in countries they traded with, whereas joint-stock companies frequently did. The directors of a joint-stock company do not carry out any trade personally; their interest lies in the success of the company's general trade, which goes hand in hand with maintaining the forts and garrisons necessary for its defense. The directors of a joint-stock company manage a large amount of capital—the joint stock of the company—a portion of which they employ in building, repairing and maintaining these forts and garrisons. The directors of a regulated company, on the other hand, do not have this capital, their income consisting of revenue from admission fees and corporation duties imposed on the company's traders.

In 1750, a regulated company was established to maintain all of the British forts and garrisons located between Cape Blanc and the Cape of Good Hope, and later on those located between Cape Rouge and the Cape of Good Hope. The company was prohibited from exporting Negroes from Africa or importing any African goods into Britain; however, since they were responsible for the maintenance of forts and garrisons, they were allowed to export certain commodities from Britain to Africa. Parliament allocated the company an annual sum for the maintenance of the forts— generally about £13,000. The captains of his majesty's navy and any other commissioned officers appointed by the board of admiralty were allowed to inquire as to the condition of the forts and garrisons, and report their observations to their board. The garrisons of Gibraltar and Minorca were originally established to protect Mediterranean trade.

The trade of a joint-stock company is always managed by a court of directors, but the total exemption from risk beyond a limited sum incited many an entrepreneur to join these companies. The trading stock of the South Sea Company at one time amounted to over thirty-three million eight hundred thousand pounds. The capital of the Bank of Britain amounts at present to ten million seven hundred and eighty thousand pounds. Joint-stock companies for foreign trade have seldom been able to compete against private entrepreneurs. They seldom succeed without the grant of a monopoly – and frequently fail even if they have this.

The Hudson's Bay Company exclusive charter has not been confirmed by act of parliament. The South Sea Company, as long as they remained a trading company, were granted a monopoly through an act of parliament; so, too, was the United Company of Merchants, which trades to the East Indies.

The Royal African Company soon found that they could not maintain competition against private entrepreneurs, and in 1732 they resolved to sell the Negroes they had purchased on the coast to companies trading to America.

The Hudson's Bay Company had been much more fortunate. No private entrepreneurs ever entered into competition with them to that country.

The South Sea Company had a huge amount of capital divided among a huge number of proprietors. It was naturally to be expected, therefore, that there would be some recklessness and negligence in the management of their affairs. The first trade they engaged in was that of supplying the Spanish West Indies with Negroes, but both Portuguese and French companies had been ruined by this trade. In 1724, the company ventured into the whale fishery business; however, only one of the eight journeys their ships made to Greenland made a profit. In 1722, the company's immense capital of thirty-three millions pounds was lent to government; an end was put to their trade with the Spanish West Indies, and the company ceased operations as a trading company.

The old English East India Company was established in 1600 by a charter from Queen Elizabeth, after which it traded successfully for many years. In 1698, a new East India company was established. Competition between the two companies and with private traders ended up destroying both. In 1702, the two companies were united by an indenture tripartite, to which the queen was the third party. During the French war that began in 1755, East India shared in the general good fortune of Britain; they defended Madras, took Pondicherry, recovered Calcutta and acquired the revenues of a rich and extensive territory.

The only areas of trade a joint-stock company can carry out successfully without the grant of a monopoly seem to be those in which operations can be standardized, such as banking, insurance against fire, sea and capture during wartime, construction of navigable canals, and water supply businesses.

Of the Expense of the Institution for the Education of Youth

Educational institutions can be managed in such a way as to largely carry their own costs. In every profession, an individual's motivation is driven by need; those whose salaries are their only source of survival will be more motivated to perform well.

In some universities, teachers' salaries are supplemented by tuition fees paid by students. Reputation remains important to these teachers, who are motivated towards excellence by the results achieved amongst their students.

In other universities, a teacher is prohibited from receiving any fee from his pupils, and his salary constitutes his entire revenue. If his salary remains the same whether or not he performs well, he is likely to cut corners and work as little as possible. If the school is regulated by a minister of state, he is not likely to abuse his position totally, but all that such superiors can force him to do is give a certain number of lectures.

Europe's universities were originally instituted to educate churchmen, with theology the principal subject. A corrupted form of Latin had become the common language throughout Western Europe, and was used in church services and translations of the Bible read out in church. Over time, however, this language gradually ceased to be used in Europe.

European universities saw metaphysics as a more useful science than physics. The proper subject of experiment and observation, a subject in which careful attention often led to useful discoveries, was almost entirely neglected. Though universities were originally intended only for the education of churchmen, they gradually opened their doors to other students, most of whom were wealthy gentlemen. The majority of what is taught in universities, however, is not geared towards the world of business.

In Britain, it became customary for young people to go off on a sabbatical break after leaving school, travelling abroad in order to widen their horizons. A young man, however, would commonly return home incapable of serious application to either study or business. Spending years away, free of parental control, they often go off the rails. Nothing can have a worse effect on young people than this absurd practice of a sabbatical at this young age.

There are no public educational institutions for women, who tend to be taught just what their parents or guardians believe is necessary. This education generally focuses on useful life skills such as preparing them for marriage and motherhood.

Division of labor, which touches the majority of the population, is such that it is intellectually confining, since a worker will generally repeat just one or two actions all day long and is therefore not mentally stimulated. His dexterity in his trade comes at the expense of his intellectual virtue.

The wealthy are not affected by this phenomenon as they generally do not start their professional lives until the age of eighteen or nineteen, and as such have plenty of time to acquire useful life skills, often supported financially by their parents or guardians. This is not the case for the less wealthy, who are obliged to enter the workforce as early as possible in order to make a living, which leaves them little leisure time. The essential aspects of education, however—reading, writing, math— can be acquired at an early age, before students start their working lives. As such, schools should be established in every parish, in which children can receive education for a small fee, so that even the working classes can afford it. In Scotland, nearly the entire population has been educated in such establishments.

Of the Expense of the Institutions for the Instruction of People of all Ages

Religious educational institutions traditionally focused not so much on making people good citizens in today's world, but more on preparing them for the afterlife. Teachers' salaries were paid either through voluntary contributions from their audience or a fixed salary or stipend. In every hierarchical society, there are always two different systems of morality: one strict, the other liberal. The liberal system favors the pursuit of pleasure—contrary to the austere system, which abhors such behavior. For the common laborer, a single week of such behavior can cost him his job; the wiser among them avoid such excesses.

Almost all religious sects are started by the lower classes, from whom they generally draw their earliest proselytes. These sects exercise an austere system of morality. Whereas a common laborer living in a small country village is likely to be known and respected by his fellow villagers, in a large city he will just be one of the masses, unnoticed and uncared for. Individuals in this situation often seek a sense of belonging and respect by joining a religious sect. They will be required to adhere to strict moral codes within the sect, and failure to do so resulting in expulsion. One way of decreasing the unsocial and extreme behaviors promoted by these sects is through the study of science and philosophy, or encouraging people to pursue cultural activities such as painting, poetry, music, etc., which dissipate melancholy and gloom.

The clergy of every established church constitute a great corporation. Their interest as an incorporated body is never the same as that of the sovereign, and is sometimes directly opposed to it. Their main concern is to maintain their authority over the people, which the do by promoting faith as a means of avoiding eternal misery. The authority of religion is superior to every other authority, with the fears it instigates conquering all other fears.

In the ancient state of Europe, the wealth of the clergy gave them the same sort of influence over the common people as that of the great barons over their subordinates. The estates granted to the church established jurisdictions that did not fall under the king's authority.

The church's revenues exceeded what the clergy could consume, and the surplus was employed in charity work. With the gradual advancement of the arts, business and commerce, however, the church's charity work and hospitality gradually decreased. Their tenants started to grow independent of them, with the lower classes no longer reliant on them as they had been in the past. The power of the church was reduced to their spiritual authority, which itself was greatly weakened as its charity work diminished.

The reformation began in Germany and soon spread through every part of Europe. The followers of Luther, together with what was known as the Church of Britain, exercised episcopal government. This system of church government promoted peace, good order, and respect of the civil sovereign. The followers of Calvin, on the contrary, allowed the people of each parish to elect their own pastor and established equality among the clergy.

In Presbyterian churches, where patronage is respected, the clergy endeavor to gain the respect of their superiors through their knowledge, irreproachable lifestyle and diligent work. Indeed, the Presbyterian clergy of the Netherlands, Geneva (Switzerland) and Scotland are some of the most respectable men in the Europe.

Benefices (the income and property provided for pastoral duties) are on the whole equal and minimal, which has a positive effect in that only exemplary morals can give dignity to a man of low income. People tend to view a pastor with the kindness with which we normally view someone in similar circumstances to our own, but whom we think ought to be in a higher position. Their kindness naturally encourages his kindness, and he strives to assist them.

In countries in which church benefices are very moderate, a chair in a university is generally a better establishment than a church benefice. The universities have, in this case, the picking of their members from all the churchmen of the country, who are all highly educated. Where church benefices are more substantial, the church naturally draws their educated clergy from the universities. In Britain, the church continually drains universities of their most educated members; whereas in protestant countries, the most educated men will have been professors in universities.

## Part IV

Of the Expense of supporting the Dignity of the Sovereign

The expense of supporting the majesty or dignity of the sovereign is naturally high, since we expect the king to live in splendor.

## Conclusion

The general expense of defending a society, administration of justice, maintaining good roads and communications, institutions for education and religious teaching should be supported by the whole of society in the form of taxes, with local expenses being supported by a local revenue.

The general revenue of society must make up for the deficiency of revenue in many particular branches of trade.

# Chapter II
## Of the Sources of the General or Public Revenue of the Society

Revenue may be drawn either from the sovereign or the people.

## Part I

Of the Funds, or Sources, of Revenue, which may peculiarly belong to the Sovereign or Commonwealth

Contributions paid to the sovereign are either in the form of stock or land. With the Bank of Britain's ordinary dividend at five and a half per cent, and its capital at ten million seven hundred and eighty thousand pounds, the government could borrow this capital at three per cent interest and expect to make a profit. A mercantile business such as the post office receives an advance from the government to cover the cost of establishing the various offices, which it repays with hefty interest rates.

The Government of Pennsylvania implemented a method of lending at interest on land, via transferable bills of credit that are declared legal tender. This raised about £4,500 annually in government contributions.

The most significant expense for any state is war—contrary to the administration of justice, which is a source of revenue, and farm labor during harvest time, which covers the expense of constructing and maintaining the country's bridges, highways and other public works.

The revenue derived from land comes mainly from the produce of the land rather than its rent. Britain's ordinary revenue amounts to over ten million a year. But the land tax, at four shillings, amounts to less than two million a year. Britain's crown land does not bring in any revenue—which it would if privately owned; if crown land became private property, it would be cultivated, increasing produce and ultimately resulting in population growth and increased revenue for the country.

In this light, it would be preferable for crown land to consist only of parks, gardens, public walks, etc., which cost society rather than bring in a revenue.

## Part II

Of Taxes

Individuals' income comes from three different sources: rent, profit, and wages—all of which are subject to taxes.

Four maxims:

1. Inhabitants of a state must contribute towards the support of its government by paying income tax.

2. Taxes are fixed and not arbitrary.

3. Taxes should be levied at a time and in a manner convenient to the contributor.

4. An injudicious tax system results in a temptation to smuggle; the law creates the temptation then punishes those who yield to it.

# Article I

Taxes upon Rent—Taxes upon the Rent of Land

Tax on the rent of land can be levied at a blanket rate for each district or a variable rate in proportion to the rent of the land.

A blanket rate land tax for each district, although equal at first, will grow unequal over time. The advantage for landlords in Britain of a fixed, constant rate for land tax is that land has been improved and hence increased in value; consequently the rent for land has also increased.

Economists in France believe the most equitable system is one of land taxes on the rent of land, which vary in line with the rent or in line with the level of cultivation.

In Venice, all arable land leased out to farmers is taxed at a tenth of the rent. The leases are recorded in a public register.

Some landlords request a rent in kind rather than a monetary payment; for example, corn, cattle, poultry, wine, oil, etc.; others prefer a rent in service. Such rents are always more harmful to the tenant than beneficial to the landlord, with these tenants tending to be poverty-stricken.

In terms of improving land, landlords should be encouraged to cultivate part of their own land; they can afford to experiment and make a few mistakes—and ultimately this will contribute to improving the land throughout the country.

The expenses incurred for levying a land tax that varies in proportion with rent are greater than those for a tax based on a fixed rent. Land taxes that vary according to the level of cultivation of the land are not advisable because such taxes prompt the landlord to increase the rent, thus making both landlords and tenants less likely to cultivate their land

and ultimately discouraging productivity. Land taxes should be managed in such a way as to encourage cultivation of land.

Taxes that are Proportioned not to the Rent but to the Produce of Land

Taxes levied on the produce of land are taxes on the rent. When a proportion of the produce is to go towards paying tax, the farmer calculates in advance what this amount is likely to be—just as he calculates the 10% church tithe. The tithe is an unequal tax since the church takes a large share of the profit yet pays nothing towards the farmer's expenses.

Taxes on the produce of land are levied either in kind or money. The parson of a parish or a man with a small income living on his own estate has the option of being paid in kind, relying on his tithe, or charging rent.

Taxes paid in money can be variable, fluctuating in line with the market, or fixed; for example, a bushel of wheat always valued at the same price.

Taxes on the Rent of Houses

The rent of houses can be taxed either on the rent of the land on which the building is constructed, or on the rent of the building itself.

The rent paid for the building should cover the amount of interest the owner would have made had he lent it upon good security, as well as the maintenance costs. The rent of the building, or the ordinary profit, is therefore regulated by the ordinary interest of money.

Rent of the ground upon which the building is constructed is generally highest in a country's capital and other regions in which housing demand is high.

A tax on house rent, payable by the tenant in proportion to the rent, does not affect the building rent. Whereas the poor spend the majority of their income on food, the wealthy tend to invest in costly homes. Taxes on house rent therefore affect primarily the wealthy, and are comparable to a tax on a commodity.

Landowners seek to charge as much as possible for renting out their ground. In Britain, the rent of houses is supposed to be taxed in the same proportion as the rent of land, through the annual land tax. This has always proved an extremely unequal taxation system.

## Article II

Taxes upon Profit, or upon the Revenue arising from Stock

Profit from stock can be divided into two parts: the interest made by the owner of the stock, and a very moderate compensation he receives for the risk and trouble of employing the stock. The employer must receive this compensation, otherwise he would not be able to continue.

At first sight, interest made on money seems to be as suitable for tax as the rent of land. There are, however, two different circumstances to consider.

First, the quantity or value of land owned by a man can never be kept secret from the authorities—unlike the capital of stock. Enquiries into individuals' private circumstances would cause public outrage.

Secondly, land is immovable, whereas stock can be easily moved from one country to another. Owners of stock may opt to move from a country charging hefty taxes to one with tax laws more favorable to his business, thus enabling him to enjoy a better lifestyle. By moving his stock, he puts an end to all the business it maintained in his original country.

Taxes upon the Profit of particular Employments

In some countries, taxes are imposed on particular branches of trade. In Britain, these include hawkers and peddlers, horse-drawn coaches and places in them, and publicans, who are required to purchase a liquor license.

Taxes on the profits of a particular branch of trade are not charged to the traders but to the consumers, with the tax included in the price of the commodity. Consequently, consumers tend to buy large quantities rather than small, which can have a negative affect on the small trader. The tax of five shillings a week charged on every horse-drawn coach, and ten shillings a year on a seat in these coaches is proportionate to their sales volume, and consequently does not encourage bulk buying and harm the smaller trader. The tax of twenty shillings a year for a license to sell ale, forty shillings for a liquor license, and forty shillings more for a wine license, being the same price for all retailers, necessarily favors bulk buying and affects small traders.

The poll taxes charged in the southern provinces of North America and the West India islands are annual taxes charged per Negro, and as such can be viewed as taxes charged on a certain species of stock employed in agriculture. As the majority are planters, both farmers and landlords, the final payment of the tax falls upon them in their capacity as landlord.

## Appendix to Articles I and II

Taxes upon the Capital Value of Lands, Houses, and Stock

While property remains in the possession of the same person, taxes will not decrease its capital value; however, when property changes hands—for example, property inherited following death, or property sold to another individual—the taxes imposed will decrease its capital value.

All taxes on the transference of property decrease the capital value of that property and increase the revenue of the sovereign, at the expense of the people.

Stamp duties on cards, dice, newspapers and magazines, etc., are taxes on consumption. Taxes on the transference of property are quite different. The transference of property, be it through inheritance or the sale of land and houses from one individual to another, are public transactions and are taxed directly. The transference of stock from individual to individual is frequently conducted in secret, and is taxed indirectly via a stamp duty on the deed (which is otherwise not valid) as well as a requirement that the transfer be recorded in a register, for which certain duties are charged. Stamp and registration duties are also often imposed on deeds transferring property through inheritance or sale. In Britain, stamp duties are calculated in proportion to the deed, and do not generally exceed six pounds.

## Article III

Taxes upon the Wages of Labor

A person's income is regulated by the labor market and average prices of consumer goods.

Employers pay a direct tax for each laborer they employ. A manufacturer will offset this tax by charging a higher price for his goods; consequently, the tax is ultimately paid by the consumer.

A direct income tax results in lower prices for rent of land and higher prices for manufactured goods than would have been the case for tax on the rent of land and consumable commodities.

Direct income tax sometimes results in a significant fall in the labor market, industry decline, lack of jobs for the poor, and a drop in the country's annual produce of land and labor.

## Article IV

Taxes which it is intended should fall indifferently upon every different Species of Revenue

Capitation Taxes

Since a man's fortune fluctuates, it is difficult to establish an accurate estimate without an official investigation; assessment is therefore arbitrary. Whether a tax is light or heavy, uncertainty always causes grievance.

Poll taxes, when levied rigorously, provide substantial revenue for the state; however, this is a part of the public revenue and therefore not the most beneficial for the people.

Taxes upon Consumable Commodities.

The impossibility of levying tax in proportion to revenue led to taxes being levied on commodities. Consumable commodities can be classed as essentials or luxuries.

Essentials are not only the basics indispensable for survival, but also items deemed necessary by a particular culture; for example, a linen shirt is not indispensable for survival but forms an integral part of a businessman's work attire. Leather shoes are deemed a necessity in Britain; whereas in Scotland they are only deemed necessary for men, and it is not unusual to see women walking about barefoot. Beer and alcohol can be classed as luxury goods; a man can abstain totally from them and in no culture are they viewed as a basic essential.

Wages are regulated by the labor market and the price of basic essentials. A tax on these articles raises their price, and should therefore go hand in hand with a rise in workers' wages.

This is not the case with taxes on luxury goods. An increase in their price does not incur any rise in workers' wages. A tax on tobacco will not raise wages, despite the fact that in Britain it is taxed at three times, and in France at fifteen times its original price—likewise with taxes on tea and sugar, which in Britain and the Netherlands have become luxuries amongst the lower classes.

Taxes on luxury goods do not tend to raise the price of any other commodities—whereas taxes on essentials, by raising the wages of labor, automatically raise the price of the commodity, consequently decreasing sale and consumption.

In Britain, the major essential goods that are taxed are salt, leather, soap, and candles. Salt is taxed at three shillings and four pence a bushel—about three times the original price of the commodity. Leather is a necessity for daily living, as is soap. In countries where the winter nights are long, candles are essential for every business. In Britain, taxes on the price of leather are at about 10%, on soap about 25%, and on candles about 15%. As these commodities are considered basic essentials, such heavy taxes increase expense for the industrious poor, and therefore raise the wages of their labor.

In a country such as Britain, where winters are bitterly cold, fuel is a basic essential, with coal being the cheapest fuel. Most businesses are located in coal counties; in some businesses, coal is a necessary tool of trade—for example, in the glass, iron, and metal industries. Legislature has imposed a tax of three shillings and three pence a ton on coal transported via the coast, which is more than 60% of the price at the pit. Coal transported by land or inland navigation pays no such duty.

The bounty on the exportation of corn raises the price of this essential commodity and as such, rather than making a profit, often actually incurs considerable expense to the government. The high duties on the importation of foreign corn, which in years of abundance amount to a prohibition, and the absolute prohibition of the importation of live cattle or salted provisions have all led to taxes being levied on these essential commodities, and provide no revenue to the government.

Taxes on meat are still more common than those on bread—perhaps because meat is not regarded as a necessity.

Consumable commodities, whether essentials or luxuries, are taxed in two different manners: either the consumer pays an annual sum (e.g., coach and plate tax), or the goods are taxed while still in possession of the dealer, before delivery to the consumer (e.g. excise and custom duty).

A coach may last ten or twelve years; it is more convenient for the buyer to pay four pounds a year than a lump sum of forty to forty-eight pounds upon purchase. In the case of housing taxes, it is more convenient to pay these in moderate annual installments than a hefty lump sum at the time of sale.

The term "*custom* duty" demotes a tax that is paid *customarily*. These taxes were originally imposed on merchants, who were disliked and whose gains were envied—for example, foreign merchants, who were taxed more heavily than their British counterparts. This distinction between the duties charged to foreigners and those charged to British traders is still practiced today, to give the British traders a competitive advantage.

These duties were first charged on wool and leather in the form of an exportation duty. Other duties included those on wine, which were charged per ton (tonnage) and on other goods, which were charged per pound (poundage).

The exportation of materials produced within a country or its colonies was sometimes prohibited and sometimes subjected to higher duties. The exportation of British wool was prohibited; that of beaver skins was subjected to higher duties (Britain having the monopoly over this commodity following its conquest of Canada).

With a number of goods prohibited altogether, smuggling is rife. Britain's ban on the importation of foreign woolen goods, and its tight restrictions on foreign silks and velvets not only prevent any revenue being made through customs duties, but encourage people to smuggle these goods in, including merchants who smuggled in as much as they could. This is a perfect example of the mercantile system being used as an instrument of monopoly rather than revenue generation.

The foreign commodities most widely consumed in Britain are wines and brandies, products from America and the West Indies—sugar, rum, tobacco, cocoa-nuts, etc.; and products from the East Indies—tea, coffee, chinaware, spices, piece-goods, etc. The majority of the country's revenue from custom duties comes from these products.

In Britain, liquor and spirits brewed for private consumption are not subject to excise duty. This exemption favors the wealthy rather than the poor, since almost all wealthy families in the country brew their own beer, which costs them eight shillings a barrel less than it costs the common brewer. As such, the wealthy are able to drink their beer for less than can the poorer classes, who tend to purchase theirs from a pub.

In addition to customs and excise duties, there are several other duties, which affect the price of goods more indirectly. An example of this is the duties imposed on the road and waterway tolls that pay for the maintenance of the road or waterway. These are calculated according to the volume or weight of the goods being transported. If Britain's road or waterway tolls were to become a government resource, with duties imposed on the value of the goods rather than their volume or weight, this inland customs and excise would damage the most important of all branches of commerce: the country's national trade.

Levying taxes on luxury goods requires a large number of customs officers, whose salaries and benefits contribute nothing to the state treasury; customs officers' benefit packages tend to amount to much more than their basic salaries—in some ports more than double or triple those salaries. The expense of levying revenue could be as much as an additional twenty or thirty per cent of these salaries and benefits.

Such taxes on commodities raise their price, thus discouraging their consumption and production. In the case of home-produced commodities in particular, this leads to a reduction in labor.

Not many people are scrupulous when it comes to smuggling; generally, if people can find an easy and safe way of doing so, they will. Shoppers are equally unscrupulous when it comes to buying smuggled goods.

Inland trade is practically duty-free, with most goods able to be transported from one end of the country to the other without any license or control by revenue officers. Goods transported from coast to coast require certificates but are for the most part duty-free, with the exception of coal.

# Chapter III
## Of Public Debts

In a commercial country, the sovereign spends a large portion of his revenue on luxury goods—often to the detriment of the state's military power. His expenditures will often outweigh his revenue, sometimes requiring him to borrow from his subjects. During wartime, most states are required to go into debt, with investments being made in increasing the size of the army, equipping fleets, and preparing garrisoned towns for defense, including the purchase of arms, ammunition and provisions. Vast amounts of capital are therefore required fast in order to prepare for war—which will not wait for the gradual returns on new taxes. The government therefore secures this capital through borrowing.

Commercial countries are home to many wealthy merchants and manufacturers, who are in a position to be able to advance large sums of money to the government. These people trust the government, since the government provides them with security and a legal system that enable them to operate their businesses. This fact, coupled with the extremely favorable loan terms offered by the government for such loans, disposes people to lend to them.

Aware that they will be able to borrow in times of need, governments of such countries often cease to manage the country's economy effectively. This results in major debts, which are likely in the long term to ruin Europe. Nations, like private men, have generally started to borrow through personal credit, without assigning or mortgaging specific funds for the reimbursement of this debt. When this system has failed them, they have started to borrow against the assignment of specific funds or a mortgage.

Britain's so-called "unfunded debt" consists of a debt that is partly at zero interest and partly at full interest—very much like a private person's contract against a promissory note. The Bank of Britain maintains their value and facilitates their circulation, which enables government to contract these large debts when needed.

When this resource is exhausted, the government turns to specific branches of public revenue in order to raise the capital it needs to repay this debt. It raises this money either as a short-term or a perpetuity mortgage. Money raised from a short-term loan is known as anticipation; that raised through a perpetuity mortgage is known as perpetual funding.

In Britain, annual taxes on loans are anticipated according to the terms stipulated in the loan's borrowing clause. The Bank of Britain lends at interest rates of between 8% and 3%. If there is a deficiency, which there always is, it is provided for in the funds for the ensuing year; the only major branch of public revenue that is still unmortgaged is therefore regularly spent before it comes in. Like an extravagant spendthrift whose social engagements do not allow him to wait for his regular salary, the state constantly borrows from its own agents, paying interest for the use of its own money.

Over time, various acts have been passed under which taxes that had previously been anticipated only in the short term were rendered perpetual, to be used to pay only the interest on the borrowed amount.

There are two other loan methods: annuity loans—either for a specific period of time or an entire lifetime. During the reigns of King William and Queen Anne, large sums were frequently borrowed in annuities for a specific period of time, both short and long term. In 1691, an act was passed enabling a million to be borrowed as a lifetime annuity (a form of group life annuity devised by Tonti) at 14%; however, such was the supposed instability of government that even these favorable terms resulted in few purchasers.

In modern governments, peacetime expenses are largely equal to peacetime revenues. When war occurs, the government is both unwilling and unable to increase its revenue in proportion to the increased expense. Increasing revenue would mean increasing taxes—which is not an option since an increase in taxes would cause major disillusionment amongst the people, with regard to the war. The government is, however, able to borrow from individuals—which enables it to raise sufficient money to fund the war, with just a moderate tax increase. Through perpetual funding, they are able to raise large amounts of money with very moderate tax increases.

Any new tax is always immediately felt by the people and will generally be faced with opposition and resistance. The more taxes are increased, the more the people object; the more loudly they object to each new tax brought in, the more difficult it becomes to implement new taxes or raise current rates.

In Britain, from the time of the first recourse to borrowing, to the ruinous practice of perpetual funding, the reduction of public debt during peacetime has come nowhere near to paying off the debt accumulated during wartime. Indeed, Britain's current huge debt dates way back to the 1668 war, which concluded with the Treaty of Ryswick in 1697.

When government expense is paid for using annual revenue from the produce of free or unmortgaged taxes, a portion of the people's revenue is just being redirected from maintaining one form of unproductive labor towards another. When public expense is paid for through funding, this draws on capital that already exists in the country—redirecting a portion of the annual produce destined for the maintenance of productive labor towards that of unproductive labor.

The latter method of funding, although depleting this existing capital, is more favorable to the accumulation or acquisition of new capital than the method of defraying public expense through revenue raised throughout the year. Under the funding system, some careful spending and diligence amongst a country's people can more easily repair the damage caused by a government's waste and extravagance.

It is said that payment of the interest on public debt is like the right hand paying the left; the money does not leave country—it is one group of inhabitants' income being transferred to another. This view suggests that the whole public debt is owing to the inhabitants of the country, which is in fact not the case; the Dutch, as well as several other foreign nations, have a considerable share in our public funds.

Land and capital stock are the two original sources of all revenue, both private and public. Although it is in a landowner's interest to maintain his estate in as good a condition as he can, the various land taxes often leave him with insufficient revenue to do so. With landowners unable to maintain their land, the country's agricultural industry inevitably declines.

When national debt accumulates beyond a manageable level, the country's economy spirals out of control, often culminating in bankruptcy and the need to tap into public revenue. Countries often disguise public bankruptcy as a "pretend payment" by increasing inflation rates. When a state or individual is forced to declare themselves bankrupt, the best policy is to do so openly and transparently; this result in the least dishonor to the debtor and the least damage to the creditor.

Almost all states, however, both in the past and today, when faced by this situation, have attempted to redress the situation through inflation: gradually decreasing their currency below its original value so that the same nominal amount gradually contains less and less silver.

Britain's public revenue can never be completely liberated since the surplus remaining after payment of annual expenses is so small as to be insignificant. The liberation of public revenue can never be brought about without considerably increasing public revenue or reducing public expense.

Commerce within the United States is conducted exclusively in banknotes rather than gold and silver, with any gold and silver that does come into their system being sent to Britain in exchange for commodities. But without gold and silver, there is no means of charging taxes; Britain receives all of the US's gold and silver—how is it possible to draw from them what they do not have?

The present scarcity of gold and silver in America is not due to poverty in the country or the inability of American citizens to purchase it. In a country where wages are significantly higher and the price of provisions much lower than in Britain, the majority of the population are in a position to be able to purchase large quantities of gold and silver should they so wish. In reality, the scarcity of gold and silver is through choice, not necessity.

Any country's domestic business can be conducted using banknotes, with nearly the same degree of convenience as using gold and silver money. The use of banknotes has proven convenient for the Americans, who are able to invest the profit made on surplus produce from the land in purchasing tools of trade, clothing, furniture, and iron needed to further improve, build and extend their settlements and plantations. Colonies' governments find it in their interest to supply their people with sufficient banknotes to maintain their domestic business. Pennsylvania derives revenue from lending money to its subjects. Others, like Massachusetts, fund extraordinary emergencies by advancing banknotes to defray public expense, which are redeemed at a later date, when convenient for the colony, at the depreciated value to which it gradually falls.

# Themes Found Throughout the Book

- Self-interest, stimulated by competition, is ironically the key to prosperity.
- When competition is not inhibited, landowners and employers use their resources to maximize profits.
- Division of labor (specialization) greatly increases productivity.
- Agriculture is not as suited to division of labor as is industry.
- Money is a convenient and transportable token representing the effects of labor; its value comes only from what it represents.
- The real price of everything is the labor involved in producing it.
- Wages of labor are regulated by competition for that labor.
- A society's main commerce occurs between the countryside and the city, with the city purchasing raw materials from the countryside, which it then transforms and sells to the countryside and foreign markets.
- All forms of interference with free trade, such as market restraints to benefit a powerful minority, ultimately act against the interests of society as a whole.

# About the Book

First published in March of 1776, *The Wealth of Nations* contained 510 pages, two volumes, with books 1-3 in the first volume and 4-5 in the second. This edition was sold out within six months and was said to have had a direct effect on government policy, inspiring the Prime Minister to create new subjects for taxation.

A second edition was published two years later. The main differences noted were in the terms applied to the American colonies, which were in process of separating from the "mother country." Some footnotes were added, and there were minor additions and alterations to the text, but on the whole it takes careful comparison to find much difference between these editions.

Between the second and third editions, the book was discussed at the Houses of Parliament in Westminster, London, at a time when political economy was an emerging field and the simplicity of argument confused those who preferred the esoteric. Many references to Smith and his foundation beliefs were made in the Houses of Parliament in subsequent years, and his work was discussed favorably by United States President Madison.

The third edition, published in 1784, contained new material. A fourth edition followed in 1786 without significant alterations, and the fifth in 1789 was the last during Smith's lifetime. There have been a number of editions since that time, but without any additions or alterations other than commentary.

# About The Author

An early pioneer in the intellectual field of political economy, Adam Smith was born in Scotland in 1723. His father was a lawyer, but died a few weeks after his son was born (although some report the birth was after his father's death), which must certainly have affected his upbringing by his widowed mother and probably brought them that much closer together. His mother is credited with encouraging his scholastic tendencies.

At age 14, he entered the University of Glasgow, after which he was awarded a scholarship, funded by a Glaswegian, to attend Oxford University, where he spent six years. His evident contempt for the professors of that university suggests that he was not happy there. He later returned to Scotland, where he proved a popular lecturer in Edinburgh at a time when people went to lectures as a form of entertainment. He was subsequently appointed Professor of Logic then Professor of Moral Philosophy at his former University of Glasgow. His first book, *The Theory of Moral Sentiments*, focused on moral philosophy and examined the nature of empathy. In 1762, the University of Glasgow conferred on Smith their honorary title of Doctor of Laws (LLD).

Despite his chronicled contempt for salaried teachers, he quit the university in 1764 to accept a job as a tutor to the boy who was to become Duke of Buccleuch. He later received a comfortable pension from that family, which enabled him to travel throughout Europe, where he met other intellectuals with similar interests. During this time (1766 and 1776), he amassed and wrote the material for the book that became universally known as *The Wealth of Nations*.

In 1777, he was appointed to a government post that was compatible with his interests, as Commissioner of Customs for Scotland. At this time, he lived with his mother in Scotland's capital, Edinburgh. He was appointed Lord Rector of the University of Glasgow, a post he held from 1787-9. Adam Smith died in Edinburgh in 1790 without ever having married.

Made in the USA
Coppell, TX
29 April 2021

54700536R10066